Over The Edge:
How One Woman Learned To Channel The Universe

CHRISTINA LOPES

DEDICATION

To Bernie, Idalina, and Carlos. Thank you for our journey together. How I love you.

Some names have been changed in order to protect the identities of those involved. All changed names are noted with an asterisk.

CONTENTS

INTRODUCTION

Imagine standing on a stage in a filled stadium. Someone passes you a microphone. You know that whatever you say will be heard all over the stadium and perhaps beyond. Now, imagine you can only say one full sentence before the sound is turned off. What would you say? What would be the most important thing you could tell a stadium full of people?

This book is about finding that one sentence. I now know exactly what I would say. But it has taken me years and a tremendous amount of effort to understand my message. I hope the words contained herein can serve as a compass of sorts—so that you may find your one sentence without traversing the same roads I did.

The truth is, finding that one sentence you would share with a stadium full of people may completely change their lives. But most importantly, it will change yours.

PART I: THE PRECIPICE

"There are only two ways to live your life:
One is as though nothing is a miracle;
The other is as though everything is a miracle."

Albert Einstein

1 LITTLE MIRACLES

When she was small, Christina Marie intuitively understood that everything was a miracle. All of nature fascinated her. As a toddler, she would disappear into the backyard of her California home, without anyone noticing. On one such occasion, her uncle went looking for her. "Little Kool-Aid!" he shouted, using the pet name he still uses now. "Where are you?" Eventually, he came upon her, squatting in the dirt, with her back turned to him. Suddenly, she stood up, holding something delicately in her hands. Looking up at her uncle, she held her treasure and asked her most pressing question: "How does the worm know where to go if she doesn't have eyes?"

Even now, all these years later, my curiosity and love of the world around me—especially the natural realm—pervades my being. I can still feel my childish openness as if it were just yesterday. I lived life with endless enthusiasm, every new experience presenting itself as something extraordinary. Yet my open heart would also become the portal for things that would end up devastating my world many years later.

My earliest memory is one of my father carrying me in his arms while running around the house. I'm a toddler, wearing only a diaper. Around and around the house we went, my father leaping from room to room, bouncing me violently in his arms. It was fun…and terrifying, because something was wrong. Terribly wrong. As Dad dashed and leapt, my horrified mother and godmother chased him, screaming in our native Portuguese for him to stop and put me down before he dropped me. "Put her down! Please put her down!"

Their fear became my own, although I suppose I instinctively knew my father was not okay. It was only later, when I was old enough to understand, that I learned the truth of what happened that day. Although normally a gentle and kind man, he also suffered from Type 1 Diabetes, which, when uncontrolled, led to severe bouts of hypoglycemia. The result was not only shakiness, anxiety and nausea, but a delirium and confusion that changed his personality. The rational, sensible farmer was replaced by an inpatient, childish nightmare of a man who would spit in my mother's face as she desperately tried to feed him sugar cubes. And so, my first formed memory was colored by fear. Fear and I formed a bond that day, one that remained strong for many years. Now, I look back and wonder why I decided at such an early age to welcome fear as my trusted companion. Perhaps it was simply because my first memory proved to be a powerful imprint in my young brain. But by the grace of the Universe, Heaven, God (or whatever other name you may call it by), fear no longer holds me enslaved. It did, however, keep me shackled for more than 30 years.

Dad's frequent attacks would play a key role throughout my life. He was diagnosed with Type I diabetes when I was an infant, and although it was generally manageable with diet, lifestyle and daily insulin shots, he nevertheless struggled with it until it eventually took his life, at age 50. It's difficult to explain why my father struggled so much with a disease that wasn't terminal. But he did. Looking back on his key personality traits gives me a small window into his inner world. Bernie—as his American friends affectionately called him—was a dashing man. He was athletic and could have easily been a George Clooney double. Their resemblance was so striking that for years after my father's death, I felt uncomfortable watching a Clooney flick. Added to his physical attributes were traits such as loyalty, warmth, stubbornness and a good old-fashioned Portuguese macho pride. In essence, Bernie looked good to the outside world and the idea that his body could possibly be fragile scared him. I guess what it all boiled down to was that my father was deathly afraid of being sick, so he completely ignored the disease that was slowly ravaging his body. Unfortunately, insulin-dependent diabetes isn't something you can simply ignore. So when Dad decided to pretend everything was okay, that left the rest of the family to deal with his illness.

From the outside, our lives seemed quite typical of the American dream. My paternal grandmother, whom I affectionately called "Vó" (a diminutive form of Grandma in Portuguese), immigrated from Portugal's Azores islands to California in 1959. I loved her fearlessness, rugged independence and her no-nonsense way of seeing life. Vó was the type of woman who could spend hours in the backyard gently talking to her beloved chickens, then suddenly show up in the kitchen with one of them, after a quick slaughter. "She stopped laying eggs, so now I'll make some chicken soup with her." Just like that. But Vó also loved a good laugh, especially if it involved practical jokes that her children (my dad was legendary at them) played on others. It was through my paternal grandmother that I first learned not to take life too seriously. But mostly I loved hearing, over and over, the story of how this short, feisty woman ended up in America.

Imagine it's the 1950s and you're a woman. Not just a woman, but a married woman with five children clinging to your apron strings. Now imagine you live on an island in the North Atlantic, 850 miles from mainland Portugal. The islands are a place of magical beauty, but also a part of an ancient Latin culture where machismo and patriarchy dictated how men and women interacted. What's more, you're poor and despite yearning for a better life, your options are very limited. If you were my grandmother Vó, would you do what she did next? After endless discussions, arguments and plans that involved a lot of anxiety for the future, Vó used her American passport, which she had because her father worked in San Francisco during the Gold Rush of 1848-1855. It sounds easy enough to achieve these days, but back then, a mother of five who left her entire family behind to seek her fortune was the subject of criticism and suspicion. In those days, only charlatans left their husbands and only weak husbands allowed it. But Vó didn't stop to think about those things. She packed her bags and, without knowing a word of English, boarded a plane first bound for New York. Somehow, she got lost at the airport, missed her connecting flight to San Francisco and relied on the kindness of a few strangers to get her to a hotel for the night. Vó was so terrified of being in New York. Surrounded by high rises and not even understanding what an elevator was, she spent the whole night sitting on her hotel room bed, without moving. The next morning, a hotel employee was kind enough to send her off to the airport again, where she finally boarded a plane bound for California. Once there, my grandma landed a job as the seamstress, making habits for a local group of nuns who operated a charity hospital in the Central Coast. And then, one by one, her husband and children joined her. They worked hard, raised their children and later, helped raise us grandchildren from their house a few steps away from our own. Vó taught me Portuguese, how to cook and shared her recollections of her life in the Azores. My grandparent's home was always filled with music, good food, and laughter, all common characteristics of Azorean families.

Like my grandparents, my parents were hard working if uneducated people who were determined never to leave their children wanting. My father had lived in the US since he was a teenager, but Mama Idalina was "fresh off the boat." They had met in the Azores in the summer of 1976, when Dad came home on vacation, and dated long distance for a year before marrying in California. It was a completely different life for my mother, who was one of 14 children raised in abject poverty by her mother and her painfully alcoholic father. Before she arrived in the US, she'd worked long, tedious hours in a fish factory, her bare feet submerged in fish guts all day. For her, childhood was simply something to be withstood, but she would never be shy about using her experiences as a teaching tool for me and my brother Carlos. Through my mother, I learned of the burden and drudgery of poverty, the value of hard work and the even greater value of determination. My mom made a point of instilling in her two children that we could be whoever we wanted, regardless of where we came from. As I grew up and better understood the real strength she had, I knew that if she said I could achieve whatever I set my mind to, then I was absolutely going to listen to and live that truth.

Yet, behind the scenes of our regular family life was the omnipresent black cloud of my father's illness. I may never fully understand why, but he would not—or could not—better manage his condition. He neglected to monitor his blood sugar regularly, and at times, would inject himself with the wrong amounts of insulin—triggering drops in glucose that would bring on the attacks.   Even if he didn't comprehend the danger he put himself in, my mother and other adults in my life understood that a diabetic going through hypoglycemia for too long could simply slip into a coma and die. As a little girl, I didn't understand the medical aspects of his disease, but there was one certainty I felt deeply: I knew he was going to die a young man. I can't really explain how, at five, I knew this. I just did. And this "knowing" terrified me.

Of course, children can be very sensitive to energy around them, particularly the negativity that surrounded my father during one of his episodes. But sensing his fate went far beyond just 'a feeling I had.' Along with this "knowing", I had other quirks—I call them gifts now—that meant I could sense others' energy, could see and feel things that were not of this world and could understand that some people "carried" things with them that I didn't understand, but made me feel physically ill. Some children have imaginary friends and are quite happy about their encounters. Not me. I don't know what other children saw, but what I experienced terrified me. Perhaps it was because I already lived with the fear and anxiety of losing my father any day, but I realize in hindsight that I inadvertently attracted energies that were similar to my own. Without knowing it, my body was living the Law of Attraction.

The world of energy works much like meeting new people. Let's say you're at a party full of strangers and you strike up a conversation with someone. The conversation usually lasts if you find things in common to discuss. The other person becomes excited that you both share these common experiences and pretty soon…like attracts like. We bond more closely to those with whom we have lots in common. Likewise, when it came to the "world of energy" and my experiences as a young child, my body was putting out a strong fear signal and as such, I was attracting the departed souls that identified strongly with fear. I would wake up in the middle of the night—a pattern that would occur more frequently as I grew up—terrified and suffering from wrenching stomach pain. I felt exactly like the little boy in M. Night Shyamalan's movie, *Sixth Sense*. When I first saw the film, it struck a deep cord in me. It wasn't exactly fiction to me. It was a pretty accurate description of what I felt in the middle of the night as a young child. In Sixth Sense, the little boy, played by Haley Joel Osment, wakes up and feels the temperature drop in the room before he sees the souls that have come to visit him. I don't remember seeing souls in my room, but I felt a soul in the same way one can feel the warmth of a fireplace as you bring your hand close to the flames. Of course, this all makes sense to me now, but as a five-year-old, it just plain terrified me. Without making a commotion, I would quietly climb into bed with my parents. The only way to sooth my pain and fear was my father's warm hand on my tummy. I was always in awe of Dad's huge, sandpaper rough laborer's hands. Yet only these hands could calm my nightmares.

By the time I turned seven, I began to understand just how broken our family was. The increasing frequency of dad's attacks caused deep resentment in my mother. Mama was and is to this day an emotional hurricane. That is the first word that comes to my mind when I think of her. She has a soul that can move mountains and an energy so strong you can feel it from a distance. You can tell Mama Idalina is coming from a mile away because that's how far her laugh travels. Boisterous, loving, kind, strong like a rock...and wildly passionate. But my father's illness and his refusal to take care of his body caused a deep-seated, monstrous anger in her that I came to fear, too. I suspect she knew the love of her life was dying a little bit every day. She knew the damage he was doing to his body and the suffering it caused. And she hated him for it. Her anger was most apparent right in the midst of dad's attacks. He would lose his mind, run away and refuse any attempts to give him sugar. She would chase him, screaming, nervous and angry. Even as a young child, I began to see how the combination of Mama's anger and Dad's craziness actually prolonged the diabetic attacks, rather than put an end to them. It was almost as though my father, in his altered mental state, could sense my mother's rage and reacted to it by provoking her even more. At times, my grandparents or aunt would rush over to help

Mama deal with Dad.

Not surprisingly, the emotions created during Dad's health crises spilled over to everyday family life. Mere minutes after Dad would come out of a hypoglycemic upheaval, Mama would be quick to let him know just how angry she was. And the shouting would go on for a long time. My father's illness and his refusal to better care for himself was becoming a huge strain on their marriage. Sometimes, I tried to calm my mother down, just so the shouting would stop. I would slowly walk up to her and gently try to break up the fight by hugging her leg or letting her know I was there listening to it all. It was a clever little psychological trick for a small child and it did work, sometimes. But overall, my parents were too busy trying to keep their tumultuous marriage from falling apart to notice what all this trauma was doing to their children. My life felt like a land mine zone—a step in any direction could trigger an explosion. Unfortunately, all these observations and experiences laid the foundation for the development of my mental model and the closing of my heart.

2 THE ISLANDS IN THE NORTH ATLANTIC

When I was nine years old, my life took another, unexpected and not entirely welcome turn. My father decided to realize his lifelong dream and move back home to the islands he loved. My mother wasn't thrilled with this decision: the Azores were the seat of painful childhood memories that she wanted to forget. To her, the United States represented renewal and hope. It was the country that gave her financial freedom, even with a 4th grade education and limited knowledge of English. Going back to Portugal meant losing that freedom and coming to terms with her past. So why did she go? My mother has never just followed a man wherever he wants to go. I suspect she acquiesced to my father's longing because of his illness. And so we went. Yet, the decision came at a cost. Mama would go back to the Azores, but she would also always let Dad know, in her own way that she wasn't happy with the decision.

The first months on the island of São Jorge—sitting smack in the middle of the nine island archipelago—were distressing for my little brother and me. I was so angry at my father for bringing us to this place. I was hostile because he tore me away from my extended family, especially the grandparents who had helped raise me. Language wasn't a problem, since my grandparents had been instrumental in making sure I was fluent in Portuguese. The problem was everything else. The islands to this day remain a little known paradise to most of the outside world. But even the most breathtaking paradises can feel differently to those who live in them: isolating, austere, suffocating. That winter, I had my first taste of one of the most important lessons of my life: humility. In the North Atlantic, winter arrives aggressively, comprehensively and with fury. You have no choice but to see your place in the world because of Mother Nature's capacity to humble even in the most self-centered people. I remember looking out my bedroom window and seeing the immensity of that raging ocean in the winter. The size of the waves put my little ego on notice. At times, when hurricane-type storms would pass through the islands, I could hear the winds whispering to me: "Remember your place."

When Mother Nature started talking to me in her aggressive, winter language, it reminded me of my own mother's anger. It was almost as though I now had two Mama's, both of them angry, both of them shouting loudly in different languages. It just made me feel more isolated and scared. In the American suburbs, I was removed from nature. That gave my young mind some assurances that life was predictable and safe. But not in São Jorge. Being that close to nature—especially in the winter—and having lost my extended family only panicked me more. Everyone around me was a stranger and I had no one to run to other than my parents.

If winter was harsh and dispiriting, spring brought with it renewed energy and joy in my heart. After nine months of living on São Jorge, the sensitive girl who once saw the miracle in everything returned, along with the flowers, the warm sun and the open sky. The island breathed new life into me.

Mother Nature's winter language quieted to a whisper of gentle spring winds and soft rains. She wasn't angry anymore and so I looked at my island with new eyes. I excelled at school and made lots of new friends. Our little family farm was also coming along rather nicely. Dad had bought cows, pigs, goats, chickens and even a donkey! How I loved that donkey. My father understood how much I adored animals, but I think he also saw my wild side. If he bought a horse, I would probably kill myself on it. So he got the next best thing, a little brown donkey. Every day, I would race that donkey around our village of Biscoitos—roughly 300 people—and gallop into the sunset like in an old Western. But just like our family and most of the animals we owned, little donkey had a quirk: without warning or prior notice, she would stop dead in her tracks, mid-gallop. We would tear down the road at full speed and suddenly BAM... Burra (Portuguese for donkey) stopped. Since I preferred to ride without a saddle—a habit my father hated—I would shoot off the animal between her ears and land in the dirt 10 feet away. I'd get up, dust myself off, stare the donkey down and get back on. I still have no idea why the little bastard behaved that way. But I loved Burra and her quirks.

There was another reason for my change of heart about the island. His name was John Paul. JP was my cousin and lived two doors from my house. We became inseparable right away. JP was deaf, but we understood each other perfectly well. We invented our own sign language, which the adults didn't always understand. The first thing to draw me to him was that it felt as if he was a guardian angel. He had these deep brown eyes that communicated wisdom and at the same time, joy. His laughter was as powerful as my mom's—the kind of laughter that shows the beauty of your soul. JP also reminded me of my father sometimes because he, too, was a legendary prankster. Nothing would get JP laughing more than when he played a joke on someone else. That laugh. It was amazing.

As spring turned into summer, JP and I would ride

together, me on Burra and JP on his upgraded "wheels," otherwise known as a mule. She was much taller than Burra and so could gallop much faster, too. I had a hard time keeping up with JP and his long-legged beast, but we loved every minute of our rides together. Yet my connection with JP was far deeper than those wild rides. There was a kinship between us based on the mutual acknowledgement that both our families were broken, in their own ways. When we were together, I felt everything was going to be okay. John Paul was always a kind and calming soul. He was a protector. And I felt safe with him.

These moments of wonder and happiness quickly faded with the realities of family life. Moving back home had been therapeutic for my father's spirit, but it did nothing for his body. We were thousands of miles away from a quality medical system and we had lost the community of an extended family back home in the US. Once in the Azores, my father also refused to discuss his illness with anyone outside of his immediate family. That pride of his kicked into high gear, perhaps because we lived in such a small community. I could feel Dad's energy change when we moved. He felt embarrassment that his body was less than perfect. At times, I felt like I was carrying a horrible, dark secret, because it was apparent that my dad relied only on his wife and children. At the time, I didn't realize my father could have relied upon himself, should he have chosen. But he did not.

Looking back, I'm amazed that it took me years to resent my father's lack of responsibility for himself and to understand my mother's anger. Perhaps I saw him as a victim who needed care. Regardless, there were only three people in on his secret: one was very angry, one was very small and scared and one was too little to know better. That left me to be the solid buffer between a rock and a very hard place. As my father's attacks grew more frequent, I devised a system to keep the family together and protected from his episodes. When he would lose his mind and trigger a reaction from my mother, I would immediately send my little brother to his room. Then, I would place myself between my parents, absorb my mother's rage and send her away, too. When I was left alone with my father, I presented him with calm and compassion. This was no easy task for a 10-year-old. To absorb someone's anger and reflect kindness was challenging. I quickly figured out that the key to my survival was to swallow emotions and bury them deep inside. The stoicism I presented my father in his less lucid moments seemed to work. If I asked him calmly to please drink some juice or swallow a packet of sugar, he would do it. Thus I formulated my mental model: A stoic and resilient Tina.

As I became better at dealing with my father's attacks, my mother also became more dependent on me for support. I learned to be a light sleeper, should Mama come in to wake me in the middle of the night or early in the morning. I don't remember sleeping peacefully in those years. I would become most panicked during the summer and early autumn, when we would move our cattle to graze far up in the mountains. My mother and I knew that if my father had an attack up there by himself, he would die. And on one occasion, that almost happened.

It was a Saturday and I was doing what all other adolescents do at 9am on a weekend. I was still warm and half asleep but I could hear Mama coming down the hall towards my room. Something was up. "Your dad should be home by now," she whispered, so as to not wake up my brother in the next room. I quickly dressed and we drove towards the mountains. By the time we parked, my terror was alive. I knew something was terribly wrong with my father. My intuition was developing as fast as my adolescent body, even though I pushed my sixth sense away as best I could. The plot of land my family owned was heaven for cows. The lush green upper pasture made our cattle healthy and glossy, and produced top quality milk. The only downside was that it sat on the edge of a mountain, accessed by a rocky path. We either walked or rode up. Since Dad had the horse (by this time we also upgraded our "wheels"), I ran up the mountain by myself. My legs pumping and my lungs burning, I was already imagining my father dead. "This is the day," said my inner voice. By the time I reached our land, he was nowhere to be found. I took a few more deep breaths and ran back down the mountain. My heart was racing from the physical exertion and sheer terror. As I approached the road, I saw my dad being held by another man. He was soaked in mud and, strangely, milk. While out on the mountain, he had taken another turn and since he had no sugar, he resorted to the only idea his brain could consider before losing lucidity. He drank as much fresh milk as possible and passed out on the mud. Fortunately, another farmer walking on his land noticed him, hoisted Dad on his back and carried him all the way down the mountain. Another catastrophe averted—at least for the moment.

While my day-to-day family life skittered from one near miss to another, lightened by periods of relative calm and time spent with JP, I became aware that other urgent issues were surfacing. I started to notice mounting fear of the unknown, sensitivities to other realms, to energy, to things unseen by others. Already burdened with an impending sense of doom, my old friend fear cast my abilities as frightening. Every cell in my body knew that I could connect with other forms of reality, but I resisted it vehemently. I already had so much to worry about, the last thing I needed was to experience encounters with ghosts. But refusing to face reality doesn't mean it goes away.

When we first moved to the islands, my father insisted on renovating the house he was born in. He loved the home that my grandparents left him, with its solid lava rock façade, sparkling white washed walls and windows facing the Atlantic Ocean. It was charming in an Old World way, with walls so thick and solid, we could barely hear weather or passing traffic once we were inside. I guess that's why I initially felt safe there, especially during the wild winter months.

Charming as it was, it was also antiquated and needed some major modifications to bring it up to modern standards. Originally, it was built as two separate living quarters for my grandfather and his eldest sister. By the time the renovations were done, my parents had spent their life savings. To the untrained eye, the home looked new. It was also very spacious, now that the division was knocked and two houses were one. But to me, it felt old and held a very primal energy. I sensed other things living there. At the time, I didn't know how to tell my parents that I could 'feel' things. Several times a week, I would sense something lightly brush past me. I would turn to look—was it Mama?—only to realize no one was there. At other times, I just 'knew' something was in the room with me. I was just entering adolescence, so naturally, I was fearful and tried as hard as I could to close that door. But what was the door I needed to close? I didn't know, so I avoided my encounters by spending as much time as I could away from home.

Nights were particularly difficult. My room was at the end of a long hall and felt isolated from the rest of the house. Often, I would suddenly awaken to the sensation that something was trying to merge with my body. I couldn't move, speak, scream. It felt like a ton of weight pressing on my chest. It would last a few, torturous seconds and then it was gone, leaving me panicky and gasping for air. Other nights, I would awaken to the sound of my curtains moving in the wind, even though the window was closed and there was no air movement from outside. Terrified by the encounters, I started talking to whatever was present. "Please leave me alone tonight," I would whisper, like a mantra. "You scare me and I want to sleep." When the visits grew in frequency and intensity, I sought out the only person who could soothe me: my maternal grandmother. Like my mother, Grandma Carmel was a hurricane in her own right. She lived on another island, but visited us frequently. Grandma Carmel had her own interesting abilities she never discussed, but she worked miracles. She's what I call a real ghostbuster, whose gifts had been with her since she was a little girl.

3 CLOSING AND ANGER

Long before Grandma C was born on São Jorge, her position in life was determined. Her mother, Idalina, was a maid working for one of the richest families in São Jorge. In a plot worthy of a Jane Austen novel, she fell in love with the young and handsome son of the house. One day, their love found expression in a hay-filled barn and nine and a half months later, Grandma Carmel was born. Of course, it was a harsh and judgmental patriarchal society and before long, a distraught Idalina was fired from her job, then ostracized from her community. It was bad enough to be pregnant and unmarried; to be pregnant and carrying the child of a rich nobleman outraged society and placed the blame squarely at Idalina's feet, as if she was an opportunist who had seduced an unwilling and half-witted accomplice. He carried no blame, but even so, he was shipped off the island to study on the mainland, all the while denying the child was his. And so, Carmel was born with a mark already against her character. In many ways, island society never let her forget from whence she came.

Even so, growing up in these circumstances couldn't alter Grandma C's indomitable spirit. From her first steps, she was a strong spiritual being. As she grew into womanhood, her 'cleansing' rituals became known in the community. For example, if Grandma C sensed something was wrong with me, she would immediately guide me to the living room, open the windows, and direct me to sit facing away from her. As she held her rosary, she uttered a prayer which I could never decipher. As it progressed, she became ill and would sometimes gag. By the time it was all over, she was green with illness, yet I felt like an enormous weight had been lifted from my chest. Later, in her '60s, Grandma C would rarely perform the rituals, because they would weaken her and leave her unwell for long periods. Even so, she was always willing to endure the side effects for a family member. On visits, I would ask for her special prayer, not fully understanding what it was doing, but knowing I felt free afterwards, at least for a little while.

As the years progressed, spring and summer continued to be revelatory for me, as if a dark cloud had lifted and the sun was bringing hope. Every morning, I would awake with excitement. By then, my father was in the habit of bringing the pregnant cows close to home, so Dad and I could watch them before delivery. Birth is always a messy ordeal but in a cow, it's a half ton of mess. Yet watching them give birth was always a joyful moment for me. We would help the baby by roughly clearing afterbirth from his face and nose. As he took his first breaths, mama cow would already be doing what nature intended, meticulously cleaning every inch of her baby. After about half an hour, mama would gently nudge her little one, encouraging him to stand. I could sit there for hours watching this new life struggle against gravity and the ridiculously long, uncertain legs Mother Nature gave him. A few hours later, after falling on his face multiple times, the little one would be jumping around, as if he suddenly understood—legs! I get it! I have legs!—and was delighted that he knew how to use them. After being nursed for a few weeks, I'd teach the baby to drink out of a bucket. My trick was to get him drinking milk from the teat, then stick my fingers in his mouth and gently pull his head toward the bucket. At first, it worked, but that trick gets old quickly. I'd repeat the process over and over until the calf learned that there's not only milk in the bucket, but also some extra yumminess—corn meal—added to make it enticing. Pretty soon, the calves would be ready to either be sold or join our small herd.

Spring was also the time when I could ride. Dad had sold Burra and upgraded to a horse. Star was a beautiful brown mare with a white forehead marking that resembled a star, hence her name. And just like Burra, Star had an unusual quirk of her own: she was deathly afraid of rain. We could be miles away from home, but if the drops started falling, Star would head back to the barn. I would pull on the reins, scream, curse her to bloody hell and back, but it didn't matter. She just kept trotting along until she was safe from the elements. I probably owned the only horse on the planet afraid of rain. Dad didn't find it so amusing since as his working horse, she would just decide to leave whatever they were doing if she encountered inclement weather. She definitely had the spirit of a drama queen running through her. But I didn't care. My upgraded ride meant that I could possibly beat JP and his tall mule in a race. But that didn't last long. Around the same time, his father upgrade his wheels, too, and bought an enormous draft horse that was fit for a Budweiser commercial. Damn! Can't a girl have some fun?

As my little girls' body changed to that of a young woman, I felt another transformation happening inside me. The mental model young Tina had devised to keep her family together was starting to crack. I had lived with so much fear and terror from the voice in my head warning of my father's imminent death. But as hormones raged through my veins, anger and rage slowly pushed themselves to the surface. I felt an overwhelming need to explode, like I had run out of space to stuff emotions. I had reached my limit and anything could trigger an eruption. Yet, I was deeply afraid that if I exploded, I would do something unforgivable. I had no idea what it would be, but I just knew I couldn't let the cork come off the bottle, so I valiantly kept it together by tightly swaddling my heart.

But here's the funny thing about shutting a door. Nothing gets through— no love, joy, or happiness. By closing my heart, I cut myself off from the greatest of life forces. The little girl who once saw the miracle in everything was officially dead, or at least comatose for the moment. In her place was an angry teenager who presented a calm and stoic external self to the world, while suffocating my chaotic inner self.

By the time I hit my teens, things with my father had deteriorated significantly. Even though I couldn't admit it to myself, I hated him for causing us all so much pain. I loathed being his primary caretaker. And I hated God for sending me such a heavy burden. More than that, I felt deep anger because my brother had always been protected. It seemed as if he had been raised in a different family. I was the caretaker, the farm hand. My brother never got his hands dirty and would disappear from sight if things turned bad. Of course, I couldn't see that I had really facilitated my little brother's protection. I was the one who sent him away when Dad was ill and it was I who had promised to be his protector, no matter what. How could I be angry towards my parents for something I did myself? Underlying that, I also failed to see that the true source of my anger was that my parents, in allowing me to solve their problems, had abandoned me and their job as parents. Still, teenagers are masters at deferring blame. And that is exactly what I did.

Suddenly, I hated helping my father with the cows and I didn't care about riding anymore. In fact, anything farm-related embarrassed me. My father's big hands—the same hands that had soothed my tummy aches as a little girl— now looked disgusting and mangled. In him, I just saw an ignorant laborer, a man who didn't show me love or gratitude. My father was an impenetrable, concrete wall. "I can't wait to leave this house, this island," I thought frequently. Had I only known a bit more about the marvels of the universe back then, I would have noticed that my father mirrored the things I hated most in myself.

One day, Dad landed in the hospital. His kidneys were failing, leaving his limbs swollen with fluid. Doctors warned him that we had to move to one of the bigger islands, because São Jorge (pop. 9000) wasn't equipped with the dialysis machine he would eventually need. "I'm never leaving this island," he retorted. Rather than save his health, he bullheadedly vowed to remain and die on his beloved São Jorge—yet another example of Dad not taking responsibility for his life. Once his kidneys started working again after a week, he was discharged from the hospital. And he walked all the way home. It was as though he had been in jail and released into freedom. He stopped at his best friend's house for a traditional Azorean celebration of bread soup and sweet rice. Everyone there knew Dad had been in hospital, so when he showed up out of the blue, the whole place erupted into cheers and embraces. It was the first time I saw my father cry. Maybe it was so many people showing their love for him, or perhaps he was just so happy to be free and surrounded by friends and family. I watched from a short distance, stony-faced and resentful. It wasn't that I didn't want to cry—I really did—but I felt that if I let the cork come off the bottle, my anger would explode. Couldn't they see how selfish he was? Didn't they realize he was deliberately, consciously choosing his death over life with his family, despite the devastating ramifications that would have on us? I watched tears dribble down my father's face and I swallowed my own.

Although I increasingly turned inward, I found an outlet in music. It had always been an intimate part of my family life, pulsating through ours veins just as strongly as blood. My mother's family all had beautiful voices, while my father's relatives were well-known instrumentalists. I remembered Vó's house was always filled with the sound of Portuguese guitars and old Azorean songs. Yet, my parents left music behind in the US and the silence in the house was only broken by me. By age 15, I had mastered the keyboard, guitar and trumpet. I was the only girl to play first trumpet in the local orchestra, and how I ended up there reminded me of something Vó would do.

When young girls were taught to play and read music in the island school, we were generally put on to the clarinet or soprano, which were considered delicate instruments appropriate for young ladies. Somehow, they were not for me. While attending practice for the local orchestra one day, I looked over at the trumpet and thought, "That's pretty darned cool." One of the older guys who was first trumpet learned of my interest and immediately ridiculed me. "Girls don't have the lungs to play trumpet," he scoffed. That was all I needed to hear. Determined to prove him wrong and myself capable of mastering anything I put my mind to, I practiced for months, sitting at the far end of the trumpet line, about ten chairs away from him. Slowly, as I improved, the conductor moved me up the line of musicians, until one fine day I was sitting next to him. A few months later—to my macho fellow trumpeter's horror—I was officially designated first trumpet and soloist.

4 HOW HARD IS IT TO SAY "I LOVE YOU"?

Joining the orchestra also deepened my friendship with JP. Even though he was deaf and could not clearly make out musical notes, he could feel the undeniable beat of the music. Our conductor noticed this and started teaching him to play trombone. The notes would never come out in perfect pitch, but they were enough to keep beat and help our small orchestra reach a fuller sound. Still, JP struggled, so I found myself becoming his musical tutor outside of rehearsals. It wasn't all hard work. During rehearsals, John Paul's prankster personality found its voice. On break, I would set down my trumpet and run to the restroom. When our maestro called us back, I would wait for the signal, prepare to form the notes and blow…nothing. Puzzled, I would blow again. Still nothing. The maestro, annoyed that I had missed my cue, would shoot me a dirty look as I tried in vain to make a sound. I glanced over to JP, who was doubled over and nearly wetting himself giggling. Turns out, while I was out of the room, the little bastard had stuck a sock in my trumpet. And to make matters worse, the maestro would always end up screaming at me!

I had played organ for the church choir since moving to the island. It was a bit of a chore, particularly since I always felt conflicted about the Catholic Church. I loved hearing the stories about Jesus and his radical message for the times, but I resented everything else the church represented. While the priest talked about love, humility and looking inside oneself ("the log in one's eye versus the speck in another's"), after Mass, the congregation would stand outside and hypocritically gossip. It felt like those around me were merely wearing their crucifixes and going to church every Sunday more as a routine custom than because of any real devotion. Had no one paid the slightest attention to the sermon? Did anyone understand what Jesus represented when he walked the earth? To make matters worse, my father made us pray every night, forcing my brother and me to sit next to him and robotically rehash old prayers, even though he never took Communion. The whole process felt disingenuous. I would always admire Jesus' teachings, but I would never really get over my discomfort with organized religion.

One Sunday when I was 15 and playing in the church, my father had an epic attack. While I sat, bored behind the church organ and listening to yet another monotonous sermon, I sensed something was wrong. I signaled to Mama to go find Dad, who always observed Mass with a group of men at the back of the church. As I was playing the final hymn, my head was already somewhere else. As soon as Mass ended, I bolted out the door. Our car was gone. Had Mama taken Dad to the hospital? I ran in a panic, scurrying down the hill towards my house. As I approached, I could hear Mama screaming at Dad, who was in our family car. "Open this door!" she shouted, trying the locked handle. In his near manic state, he'd barricaded himself in. With every passing second of his sugar imbalance, the situation grew more dangerous. I ran up the driveway. "Mama, you must leave. This isn't helping. Please, I'll take care of it." Turning back towards the car window, I put on my soft, kind face and said tenderly, "Daddy, please unlock the door." He just kept staring ahead. An overwhelming feeling of despair and sadness washed over me. I put my head down and started to cry. I just couldn't take it anymore. As the tears rolled down my face, I looked up: "I love you, Daddy. Please open the door." Miraculously, he turned his head, looked straight at me and gently pulled the lock. It was the first time I had ever told my father I loved him. And I absolutely believe those simple, but powerful words got through to him. They bypassed his confused brain and touched his soul.

The ordeal wasn't over. Mama arrived with a glass of sugar water and gave it to me. Suddenly, my dad went crazy at the sight of the water and started running up the street. I chased him, pleading with him to stop. Every once in a while, he paused and I said my magic words: "Daddy, please drink some water." He took a big sip. I relaxed a little—and then he spit it back in my face. With that, he was off again, like a mad man. The commotion had brought the neighbors to their windows. They flicked their curtains, but no one came to help. I vividly remember one of the neighbors just standing in her window, watching our drama unfold, as if our family had become entertainment. After a few laps around the house, I finally corralled him in the kitchen, where he collapsed on the cold tiles. Sheer panic—a lack of consciousness could be life threatening. I slapped his face a few times, while Mama called the ambulance. Incredibly, he woke up before I even heard the distant sirens. "Daddy," I said, leaning over him. "I love you. Please drink." This time, he took the sugar water and drank deeply. He looked up at me. "I love you, too," he said, in a faint whisper. Another first. It was the first time he'd ever uttered those words to me.

As the sugar brought Dad back, I thought about his last words. How sad, how heartbreaking, that two people who love each other can only manage to express those feelings during a life-threatening emergency. As the days progressed after the epic episode, I heard a rumor had spread throughout our village. According to the wagging tongues, my dad had been chasing me around the house, beating me to a bloody pulp. I was so angry and hurt. My father had never laid a hand on his children, yet people preferred the made up story of child beating. That seemed to fit the narrative of our family. My father was respected and liked in the village. I was his rebellious teenage daughter. I guess it would make more sense that people believed he was beating me, rather than me fulfilling the role of a diligent caretaker. I seethed with resentment at how I had been cast. Even though I had managed to release some emotions with my tears, the cork would soon be back on the bottle. But the pressure would continue to rise within me. Maybe the pressure would one day pop the cork right off and the contents inside would come out like a volcano. I didn't know. But for now, I held it together.

Life with a closed heart is difficult. It feels suffocating, claustrophobic, lonely. Where the younger Tina could at least rely on nature, animals and music to sooth her soul, the teenaged version eschewed those pleasures. I'm not sure why I threw away the only outlets my soul had to express itself, but I did. I felt like a closet that had been packed so full, it would erupt if opened. I was a closet full of fear and pain, with no room for joy. Years later, when my life would completely implode, I wrote this poem, which encompassed my teenaged experiences.

The Soul Comes Knocking

Throughout our lives, the soul comes knocking at our door.

At first, the knock resembles a faint whisper—only perceptible to those who are awake.
Will you open the door?

If the knock goes unnoticed, it will get louder.
The sound now audible to more.

Will you open the door?

The soul will not be defeated.
Your mind—though it valiantly tries—can no longer maintain the
illusion that no one is there.
The knock soon turns to a pound.
Will you open the door?

It's getting harder to ignore, is it not?
Pound, pound, pound!
The sound is now heard by most—even if they cannot yet recognize the
guest that wishes to enter.
You see, it's not a guest at all. It's you.
You without the labels.
You without the mental movies and judgments.
It's the You that knows what is best; the You that knows its true nature.
Pound, pound, pound!
Will you open the door?

Your ego will squirm and say: "Go away, I do not wish to let you in!"
But the soul will not be defeated.
Suddenly, the pounding stops and your mind naively believes it has won.
But the silence is temporary.
CRASH!
That is the sound of your soul violently tearing down the door.
Now, you have no choice but to let the guest in.
And make no mistake: tearing down the door will cause enormous pain.
But the soul will not be defeated.

So why not open the door when the knock is gentle?
Why not welcome your guest—You—with softness and surrender, instead
of pain and suffering? Why wait for the door to be violently torn down?
Why not awaken?

I was 15. And although I had no understanding of how powerful my soul was, I did experience exquisite glimpses of my true self—the consciousness that lies at the heart of every one of us.

One day, I was milking our cows with my dad. I was annoyed that I had to be there. Dad laboriously milked cows by hand. Although it takes a great amount of wrist strength to milk, I had become quite good at it. As I sat under one of our fat cows, I was awash in rage. "I can't wait to leave this island. These stupid cows stink," I fumed. I hated cows or anything that reminded me I was a farmer's daughter. I was popular in school—part of the "cool crowd"—and it hurt that my friends were starting to crack those stupid jokes about cow shit and living off the land. They came from educated and well off families—none of whom sat under cows, pulling at their teats. "I'll die if any of my friends see me right now," I seethed.

As I immersed myself in my brooding, Dad pulled a small cup out of a plastic bag he was carrying. "Your mom packed some sweet bread today. Why don't you go eat it? I'll finish milking her." I filled the cup with warm milk straight from the cow and took my sweet bread to the top of a little hill. I was sitting on a lush pasture, surrounded by fields of blue Azorean hydrangeas, looking out toward the Atlantic Ocean. Everywhere, birds chirped and I felt the gentle touch of the onshore breeze on my skin. It was a glorious day. It was miraculous. Tears welled up in my eyes and my heart flooded with love. I looked down at my dad. He mumbled something to the cows. For a moment, I saw him as others did—the gentle, loving, kind man. For a moment, I let go and just loved my Dad.

Unfortunately, such glimpses were rare. I experienced major anxiety problems and would wake up at night with horrendous panic attacks that launched me, dry-mouthed and heart racing, out of bed. In the grip of irrational thought, I was convinced I was going to die. Fear of death—there it was again. I had transitioned from being afraid of my father dying to being panicked about my own demise. Fear, fear, fear. I was filled with it. Mercifully, my night visitors stopped coming by my room. My door to other realms seemed to have closed...at least temporarily. One less thing about which to worry.

5 THE CRASH

October, 1996.

I was 16 years old when my world was ripped wide open. It was a weekend and as usual, I was sleeping in. Through my drowsy fog, I heard howling, piercing screaming. Something was wrong. I jumped up, threw open my window and stuck my head out to locate the source of the screaming. A farmer passed in front of my house. "What's going on?" I called. He looked up and mumbled, "John Paul is dead." I staggered in shock and slumped against the wall. I couldn't breathe or utter a sound.

After a few long moments, I finally broke my silence. "Daddy! Daddy! John Paul is dead!" My father was just finishing his breakfast and my shrieking so startled him, he almost choked. I rushed past him and out into the street towards JP's house, still in my pajamas. As I reached their driveway, I spotted his parents. JP's mom was howling to the gods; his dad wept silently while holding JP's pillow. I passed them both and headed to John Paul's bedroom window. I pressed my forehead to the glass. There he was: my cousin, my best friend, my riding partner, my childhood guardian angel.

He had died in his sleep of a suspected ruptured brain aneurysm at age 17 and still looked like he was taking a nap. I stared at him for a long time, hoping this was just another JP prank and that he would soon jump out of bed and laugh at me. My breath fogged up the window. Nothing. My mom came up from behind, caressed my shoulder. "Go sit down," she whispered. "Don't look in there anymore." But I couldn't move. I watched Mama walk into the house and into JP's bedroom. Once there, she ran her fingers gently through his hair and cried. I fell to my knees and cried, too.

John Paul's death was unbearable. Not only was it painful to lose someone I loved so deeply, but the whole Azorean process of dealing with the dead made it worse. Traditional Catholic island burials must take place within 24 hours after death. It's tremendously jarring—especially when the death is sudden. One day JP was there, the next he was in his grave. I just couldn't handle the pain. Every day, I felt like I was suffocating. I couldn't breathe. Much later, I learned that living with a closed heart prevents us from processing emotions. "Emotions are energy in motion," notes Panache Desai, a wonderful spiritual teacher whose teachings and workshops worldwide have influenced me and others deeply. If we just open up and let emotions flow, our pain processes more quickly. I didn't know that then, of course. My natural, angry 16-year-old response to JP's loss was to shut down even more and shove all hurt deeper inside me. I had released some anger, some blocked energy, when I cried the day he died. But my tears were short-lived and there weren't nearly enough of them to turn the tide. Just a few days after JP was gone, I was back in my emotional prison. The darkness inside was worse. It was deep. And I could no longer even see a glimpse of anything beautiful within me.

As the last colorful hydrangeas disappeared from the rolling hills and autumn turned to winter, my panic attacks became unbearable. I couldn't tell my parents about why I awoke in a sweat at night. I was afraid of worrying my mom, who had enough on her plate in dealing with my dad. I couldn't tell my brother, who was young and self-absorbed. Nor could I tell my friends. The truth was, although I desperately needed help, I also felt a deep embarrassment about my anxiety. I was athletic and attractive, so the thought of showing weakness scared me. In fact, I was behaving toward my anxiety exactly as my father did toward his illness. So I just endured the panic attacks and became quite good at minimizing their duration. On the worst nights, I would open the bedroom window and stick out my head, hoping to get more oxygen into my lungs. The tightness in my chest was so painful that the only way I could sleep was sitting up. Laying down just felt like I was drowning in my darkness. Other nights, I would will my mind to focus on my heartbeat instead of the irrational thoughts of imminent death, and then slowly visualize it slowing down to normal. I also quickly learned that slowing down my breathing and fully exhaling my hyperventilating lungs helped ease the panic.

And then, one mid-winter night, I snapped. It happened without warning or any particular trigger. My mind just formulated this thought like a computer spitting out the answer to a mathematical problem. I sat at the edge of my bed, stared into the darkness and thought, "Dad keeps rat poison in the garage. I could drink some and this will all be over." I sat with that thought for a little while. I saw myself standing up and walking to the garage. I saw myself drinking the poison. I imagined what that would be like. Drinking poison would be a very painful way to die, but somewhere in the depths of my mind, I wanted pain. At least the physical pain would allow me to feel something. With my internal world so numb, I welcomed the idea of feeling anything. Fear gripped my guts. I was afraid of killing myself. How ironic. The one emotion that had caused me so much anguish for so many years was now the one keeping me alive. It came to me, then. Your emotions are neither good nor bad, right nor wrong. I had always thought my fear was darkness, yet now it was saving me. Isn't the universe so miraculous?

For months after John Paul's death, I teetered on the edge. Suicide never left my mind. It became the natural companion to my fear. All the chaos lived inside me. When spring came along, I again felt a little lighter with the arrival of those first sun-filled days of spring.

6 THE DESCENT INTO DARKNESS

In April of 1997—six months after JP died—my mom visited Grandma C for a few days. For all his fierce attachment to São Jorge, Dad was supportive if we needed a little break from the island, and from him. I suspect he knew how much his disease weighed on us and so was always ready to drive us to the airport or the docks. He never left the island's shores, but I remember vividly how he smiled and waved goodbye at us from the boat dock as we floated away on a ferry, bound for a camping trip or a visit with family to the larger island of Terceira. I was 17 and felt completely comfortable staying at home alone with Dad and my now adolescent brother. I was Dad's primary caretaker anyway, so it didn't matter if Mama was there or not. In fact, it felt a little liberating when she was gone. It meant I wouldn't have to absorb her anger, at least for a few days.

One morning while Mama was still away visiting Grandma C, I had a huge argument with my dad just before I left for school. It was one of those fights that starts with something insignificant and forgettable, but escalates into a firestorm. I remember that deep anger of mine surfacing quickly. Dad was sitting at the kitchen table having breakfast. My brother had already walked out the door to the bus stop. Carlos hated any type of confrontation and preferred to disappear when things got ugly. Even during heated arguments, my dad rarely raised his voice. He had this ability to control himself and bury his emotions so deep inside no one would know exactly what he was feeling. Who does that remind you of? His silence and control angered me more because it felt like he was completely ignoring me, like my feelings were of no importance whatsoever. It felt like my father only really noticed me when I was either being his farm hand or when he was in the midst of an attack and out of his mind. I threw my backpack on my back and darted for the door. But the deep anger I felt inside compelled me to turn around and say one last hurtful thing to my dad before walking out. "I can't wait to leave this house and be far away from you!" He didn't answer, so I slammed the door on my way out. As I was walking down the road to catch my bus, I could feel a small sense of relief. My tank was so full that any release of emotion or energy would instantly make me feel lighter.

Later that day, I was in the school gym, blowing off some steam. Athletics always helped rejuvenate my body and soul, particularly volleyball and soccer. As I was running around, a friend walked towards me, with a worried face. "My uncle is outside waiting for you. Your dad fell sick again and is in the hospital." I dropped everything and ran outside to the truck where my dad's best friend was waiting. The five minute ride up to the hospital felt like an eternity. Dad's friend was silent and I was immersed in my thoughts. "Boy, this must have been a bad attack for him to land in the hospital." As we pulled up, I threw myself out of the truck before it even stopped. I rushed into the ER waiting room, where several people awaited their turn to see a doctor. In a panic, I looked around and spotted the attending physician coming out of his office. "Where is my father? He came in with a diabetic attack." The doctor looked a little puzzled, then his expression changed. "Your father is dead. He's in the morgue downstairs." I couldn't breathe. The cork was coming off the bottle and I needed to be outside. As I ran out, rage emerged from the depths of my being. I made a fist and slammed it into the ER door as I left—making a thunderous sound audible through the waiting area.

Once outside, I looked up to the skies and fell to my knees. The ER doc—coincidently my father's family physician whom I mildly disliked—had followed me outside. In my agony, I actually thought he would say something soothing. Oh, how I needed to hear something human, something comforting. Yet he only confirmed why I had always thought of him as a cold, careless professional. "I understand you are upset, but there is no need to break the door." That was it. I looked up at him and asked in a quiet voice, "Can I please see my father?" He replied again with coldness. "I'm afraid not. Family members aren't allowed in the morgue." Mercifully, dad's best friend came over and helped me to my feet. He was a kind and quiet man who loved my father deeply. He was so distraught at the time that he couldn't muster up the courage to tell me himself Dad had died. I wonder if he regretted not being the person to break the news to me. Perhaps. But that exact moment served as a lesson for me. Years later, when I became a healthcare professional, I would always use this doctor's behavior as an example of what I didn't want to be. My patients and their families would always be treated with kindness.

As I headed home, the tears had dried up, but my rage bubbled just beneath the surface. It was at that very instant that I hated myself. I hated myself so deeply. Two decades later, I wrote out my thoughts on that day.

Walking Home

Walking home after my father lay dead in a hospital was numbing. My soul had known since I was a little girl that he would die young. So why was I suddenly surprised when it happened? I was numb. Numb with disbelief; numb with anger. Anger toward him for not taking care of his body and causing so much suffering to his family. And anger toward myself. Anger that of all the days God could choose to take him he does so on a day when I say horrible things to my dad before walking out the door. Sure, teenagers say horrible things when their hormones are raging and their bodies changing. But it feels devastating to say something you don't mean and know those are the last words your father hears before dying alone, in the middle of the street. What was he thinking as he passed? I hope he was feeling my love since Love transcends words. But who knows. Someday I will ask him. For me, the years that followed my father's death have served as a jail sentence for my crimes. Self-hatred was my punishment. But mercifully, the prison time is over and I am free now. Freedom has come from unconditional self-love. Finally.

Back home, I was greeted with silence. Dad's coffee mug was still sitting on the kitchen counter; his indoor sandals rested by the door. I was absolutely alone. I grabbed the phone, placed it on the dining table and just sat there for a little while staring at it. The tears began falling down my face and I cried out in despair. "Please God, help me! How am I going to tell Mama?" I rehearsed a little bit, trying to come up with soothing words that could ease the pain. But how do you tell your mother that her husband is dead? I dialed Grandma C's number and pressed the receiver to my ear. Mama answered. When I heard her voice on the line I just cried and whispered, "Mama?" That was all I needed to say. I heard the receiver on her end fall to the ground, followed by heartbroken wailing.

After I hung up, I sat frozen. My mother was on another island, four hours away by boat. I had to take responsibility for planning a funeral a mere two hours after my dad had died. It hit me again how jarring it was to bury your dead this quickly. It felt cruel, unnatural. Suddenly, the silence of the house was broken by the phone ringing. For the next hour, I sat there lifting the receiver and hearing family members cry on the other end of the line. "What happened? How did he die?" I told and retold the story about how Dad collapsed and died on the street in front our home. Our neighbor, Sara, saw him and rushed to help, but he was gone by the time she got there. It didn't sound like a diabetic attack. In fact, Dad was most likely felled by a heart attack. Neither did we ever find out—autopsies are rarely performed in Portugal where there is no suspicious circumstances. I suppose it didn't really matter, but as Sara recounted her story, illustrated with tears and wild gestures, I felt a profound agony that Dad died alone. I had always been there when he needed me. Always. Yet today, while I carried on with my day, playing sports and joking with friends, my dad lay dying in the street. Not only that but my last words to him were cruel and that deepened my agony even more.

As the news spread, our home filled up with people, the usual friends, family and villagers. In typical Azorean fashion, the food started pouring in quickly. Suddenly, the kitchen counter and dining table were filled with nature's bounty: eggs, vegetables from the neighbor's garden, coffee, fresh bread. It dawned on me how loved and respected my father was in the community. I think people also felt sorry for me and my little brother. I heard some comments about how horrible it was for us children to be alone without our mother in such tragic circumstances. As it turned out, that wasn't about to change. As people clustered around, a friend of the family rushed in to tell me all flights and ferries were done for the day. There was no way Mama could get home in time for the funeral. My heart sunk. Sensing my agony, our friend gently held my hand and said, "I will find a way to get your mother here. Even if we have to charter a damn helicopter or speed boat." His assurance made me breathe a little easier.

A few minutes later, I had more logistics to decide. Another close family friend approached me and whispered, "You have to pick a nice suit for your dad to wear and we need to decide on a coffin." I felt a deep numbness take over me. In this case, I think the numbness saved me from a complete mental breakdown at that very moment. My mind coldly got down to the business of dealing with these logistics by separating itself from the person who died. "The dead man needs a suit. No big deal." I headed to my parent's closet and just as I was rummaging through to find an appropriate "permanent" suit for my father, Carlos walked in. Someone had picked him up from school, but no one had told him what was going on. I looked at him as the tears streamed down my face, but said nothing. Finally, Carlos broke the silence. "He's dead?" Again the words just wouldn't come out of my mouth. All I could muster was a nod and some more tears. My 13-year-old brother crumbled and I felt a deep pain overcome me. I had broken my promise to him. I was supposed to be his protector, always. Yet that day I knew I was no longer able to shield him from pain. Dad was dead and nothing I could do would change that reality.

As the afternoon turned to evening, our home became the village epicenter. Dad's body lay in our living room, surrounded by older village women who prayed the rosary out loud. I couldn't bear to be in the room or anywhere else in the house, so I sat alone outside. Being under the open sky was less suffocating, less painful. I had gone into the living room earlier, when my father's body first arrived. I asked to be left alone with him and spent a few minutes in silence, just letting the tears flow. He looked handsome in the suit I had picked out. I ran my fingers through his wavy salt-and-pepper hair and whispered in his ear, "I'm so sorry, Daddy. I love you." Immediately, I felt the self-hatred again as I walked out the door crying. My mind was relentless. "No point saying you're sorry now. He's dead and you're worthless." The voice in my head had always been there, but on this day it transformed into something darker, deeper. Before, my self-loathing felt like a nuisance that was tolerated. But on this day, it became my enemy, constantly telling me how horrible I was and how I didn't deserve to be loved.

7 THE LITTLE DEVIL ON MY SHOULDER

From that point, I had a little devil sitting on my shoulder, whispering demeaning and dreadful things into my ear. I fully believed what my little devil was saying, but there was a part of me that understood the voice wasn't me. Years later, it would all make sense to me when I heard the spiritual teacher Eckhart Tolle say, "You are not your thoughts. You are the watcher of thought." Unfortunately, at 17, I wasn't ready to hear this truth. Instead, I believed the little devil's cruel words. He told me I was worthless, and that is exactly how I felt.

As the sun set over the Atlantic, I sat outside by myself. Our friends had tried desperately to get my mom home, but the high winds and violent seas overturned their plans. I looked out at those large waves and felt so insignificant again, just as I had when I first moved to the Azores as a little girl. I understood, then, how much I needed my mom. I needed her that day and on so many other days before. For years I had felt a deep and odd loneliness, a loneliness for someone who was physically, but not emotionally, present in my life. Now I completely acknowledge that I, too, had decided to remove myself emotionally from the equation. I, too, shared the responsibility for feeling alone. I had decided to isolate myself in my own chaotic internal world. But that truth only sunk in many years later. On that day, my loneliness was excruciating. It was also mixed with anger and resentment. I searched for ways to deal with these powerful emotions. I thought, "I will never let this anger go until Mama begs for my forgiveness for letting me take on the responsibility of caring for Dad." My teenage self didn't yet recognize the fundamental truth that we are each individually responsible for what we say, what we feel and how we behave. Once we understand and decide to live by this truth, nothing that occurs externally can rock our boat. I was so immersed in my thoughts and holding on to the little devil on my shoulder that I failed to recognize others had their devils, too. In essence, we all behave and engage with the world based on our mental models. So perhaps forgiveness isn't even necessary after all. "You can forgo forgiveness when you understand why somebody did something," says spiritual writer, Neale Donald Walsch. Unfortunately, on the day my father died, I had little understanding of so many things. So I just kept tight to the little devil.

As the night progressed, I learned that Mama was getting on a ship bound to São Jorge. My uncle was a sailor and had managed to call in a favor from some colleagues. There was one last boat leaving Grandma C's island that day, a cargo ship filled with consumer goods. Passengers weren't allowed on commercial vessels, but my uncle worked his magic and got Mama on board. She spent the next eight hours on high sea, suffering from violent sea sickness and heartache over the loss of her love. I was so thankful to my uncle, but I could feel Mama's agony. As I looked out at the size of the waves over the Atlantic, I felt deep pain knowing my mother was floating helplessly on those angry waters. I wasn't just imagining her pain. My body was picking up on her agony from afar. It felt like I was on that boat with her. I didn't think God cared much about me or our family, but I still tried to ask for a small favor. "Please have mercy on Mama and get her home safely. I beg of you."

I spent the time waiting and sitting outside. We lived in the mountains, so the view was quite breathtaking on most days. But that night, I didn't see the beauty of my subtropical surroundings. I saw the violence of Mother Nature, her fury. The moon was bright enough for me to see the ocean clearly and with each passing hour, I felt panic rising. My mother has always suffered from severe motion sickness, the kind that doesn't always respond to pills. Since she had boarded the boat so quickly, there was no time to get the medication that could help her weather the seas. With each breaking wave, I could imagine the violent waves of sickness assaulting her.

Mama arrived in the pre-dawn hours. When I saw the car stop at the bottom of our driveway, my heart felt a strange mixture of relief and agony. She couldn't get out by herself— the rough ocean had taken everything from her—so my aunt and uncle wrapped her arms over their shoulders and carried her up the driveway. I embraced her tightly. She collapsed on top of me and I felt thankful to feel her weight. I couldn't carry her pain, but I could at least help carry her. As disabled and dehydrated as she was, she refused my attempts to get her to bed. She insisted on seeing my father's body in the living room. I couldn't bear that sight, so I gave her to my aunt and uncle again and ran outside. A few seconds later, I heard her screams break the silence of the night. I covered my ears, dropped to the ground and cried. It was excruciating to lose my father, but it was worse to witness my family's pain. I'd always been the caretaker. But the pain of loss is one that just cannot be taken away or lessened. We must endure it on our own.

When the first rays of light emerged over the mountain tops, our home was filled with people. I had tried to get some sleep, but with the scent of fresh coffee in my head, I went to the kitchen, first stopping off at Mama's room. She'd finally been convinced to rest for a little while. But even in her sleep, she was still crying, tears streaming out of her closed eyes. By the time it came to leave for the funeral, I could sense Mama was not physically or psychologically able to go. I sat on the edge of her bed. "Mama," I whispered. "It's okay if you can't come. Carlos and I will be okay." She starred at me for a bit— her eyes were sunken from dehydration and pain. Finally, she gave me a nod and a hug. She knew she wouldn't be able to endure the funeral and felt lighter that I had relieved her of that burden. When the funeral procession passed by our house on the way to the cemetery, I could again hear Mama's agonizing wails emanating from her bedroom.

The months after my father's death were excruciating. We took no comfort in each other, but rather seemed to close our hearts and suffer alone. I couldn't look at my brother without being reminded of my broken promise to protect him. As for Mama, I was still angry at her and she was still angry at Dad. All these emotions stuck inside of us made for a rather lonely existence. We had slowly sold Dad's business. The cows went first, then the pigs and the farming equipment. Our land was rented to other farmers and their cattle was now sustained by the lush green grass. On some mornings, I would awaken to the familiar sound of cows mooing and would rush to my bedroom window in hopes of catching a glimpse of my father's beloved cows grazing on our land. But the cows mooing belonged to someone else and the nostalgia just brought tears to my eyes.

With my father's passing and no more worries about pending attacks to trouble me, I thought I would finally be able to sleep restfully. Instead, fear and panic held me fast. I had lost two of the most important people in my life in a very short period and that reality jarred me to my core. Who else would die? Who else would leave me? The little devil on my shoulder kept whispering incessantly. "Everyone leaves you because you are worthless." Every night, I would wake up in a panic and rush to my brother's room just to see if he was breathing before checking on Mama. I stood by their beds and watched them sleep for a little while to make sure God didn't decide to take them suddenly.

As the summer progressed, I decided to leave the islands. Part of me felt terrible for doing it—for leaving my mom and brother so soon after my father's death. But I was suffocated by my pain. São Jorge felt like a prison. I felt like I was on Alcatraz and needed to escape. I naively believed my prison was my physical location and that moving to the US was my ticket to freedom.

8 CLOSING MY HEART OR THE ILLUSION OF FREEDOM

So many of us repeat our patterns unwittingly, without thought. We move, change jobs or find a new spouse because we believe our prison is outside of us. We think we are suffocating because of our wives or husbands or co-workers. Yet, oftentimes, we suffocate in the prison that is ourselves. What suffocates us is not what lies externally but rather the mental model that we have built to navigate this world. The model is always built according to past experiences. Even so, you cannot run from your mind, from your ego, from the little devil on your shoulder. What really happens when you make a change to your external environment is that you feel temporary relief. You feel a false sense of freedom. But that quickly fades and you are then back to feeling suffocated and in jail again.

Sometimes it takes a whole lifetime to realize that we have spent our lives changing our external environment in the hopes of being happy. Yet what we end up doing is just carrying our prison everywhere we go. And that is exactly what I was doing when I sat on a plane bound for the States. I was finally going to be free of it all: my fear, my panic, my prison. I was 17 and so naïve.

When I arrived, I felt excited at my freedom. I was no longer a farm hand, no longer Dad's caretaker, no longer Carlos's protector and no longer Mama's anger sponge. I moved in with my paternal grandmother, Vó, and her eldest daughter, who still owned the Nipomo, California home I had known so well as a child. I quickly found a job as a therapy aide in a rehab clinic and also enrolled in the local community college. My minimum wage job brought me joy and I was helping people recover from injuries. It seemed to fit my essence as a caretaker. As the patients at our clinic got better and many of them recovered fully, I also developed a new sense of purpose. I may have failed at helping my father, but now I was successfully helping others to heal.

School was initially very difficult since my command of English was no longer strong, so I worked and studied incessantly. My little devil used my rocky start in college to come up with a new line: "You're dumb." The only way to quiet his voice was to push myself every day. After work and a day spent at school, I would lock myself in my study room and emerge only in the wee hours of the morning. My life became a constant fight to prove the devil wrong. Perhaps I would feel better about myself if I became one of the only college-educated members of my family. Perhaps I would be worthy of love if I accumulated enough money. I was very busy trying to make my external world conform to what my mind thought would make me happy and worthy. But with each passing day, that sense of suffocation crept in. My fear was still there. My sense of worthlessness was there, too. Here I was thousands of miles away from what I thought was my prison and I still felt trapped.

My sleeping patterns didn't change, either. Now, instead of being afraid that my mother and brother would die, I felt panicked about Vó and my aunty. I would get up in the middle of the night to check if they were breathing. The suicidal thoughts came back, too. One night, I realized that I felt exactly the same as I had on the islands. My external environment had changed, but I hadn't.

One night, I got up to check on them. They were both breathing and sleeping peacefully. On my way back to my bedroom, I snapped again. I can't recall what happened to trigger it, but I found myself standing in the bathroom holding a large bottle of Advil. The bottle wasn't full but its weight suggested there were enough pills to do some damage. "I wonder how many pills I need? Wouldn't want to wake up in a hospital. How embarrassing." Finally realizing that my prison was inside me hadn't helped sooth me one bit. If my prison was my mind, then how on earth would I be free of it? The only rational choice I could conceive of was to end it all. My mind would finally shut the hell up if I was dead. As I opened the pill bottle, a deep fear came over me again. Just like before, I was afraid of the act. I stared at the bottle for a few minutes and put it back in the medicine cabinet. Once again, the emotion that had tortured me for years was now keeping me alive.

Back in my room, I sat in bed for a while, staring into the darkness. If I wasn't going to kill myself, how on earth would I live the rest of my life? I decided to devise another clever mental model that would help me survive, just as I had as a child. I was only going to allow myself to feel this fear of loss for family members. They were already in my life and I couldn't do anything about that. But I swore to myself that I would never feel this agony for anyone else. I decided to close my heart and prevent it from feeling love. Without love there would be no fear of loss and I could at least survive.

9 REINFORCING THE LEFT-BRAIN

With each passing year, my world became more left-brain dominated. I discovered I was smart and took pride in having a high GPA throughout college. I decided to become a physical therapist and, at 24, moved to New York City to pursue a doctorate degree at New York University. I tried to go home to the Azores every summer. With time, distance and maturity, the islands represented freedom and I longed to be there often. My body and soul missed the breathtaking beauty, the Atlantic Ocean in all its glory. We only learn to appreciate something when we lose it and that was certainly true for me when it came to São Jorge. I finally understood my father and his love for that paradise. When I went home, I could feel the happy little girl bubbling up again, the one that knew everything was a miracle. She came to life on that island every summer. But I still carried so much pain, most noticeably when I was around my mother. Being home opened up those old wounds and as the days progressed, would bring my anger to the surface. I also sensed that Mama's anger was still there, but now it directed against life in general.

She had lost her husband at the age of 40 and was now living her life on the very island she never wanted to live on the first place. Her husband was gone, yet she felt trapped by insecurity, despite working as a supervisor for a non-profit organization that helped the poor and elderly. Sometimes, I tried to plant a seed in her mind. "Do you want to move back to the US, Mama?" I could sense her frustration in the answer. "No. I have a good job here and Carlos needs me. What would I do there now? Clean houses again? I'm getting too old for that." It's true that Carlos was going to college and that it was traditional for parents to support their children in their studies, but I felt Mama was also using Carlos as an excuse. She was simply afraid to leave São Jorge now. She wasn't happy, yet the safety of the familiar proved stronger. But her choice also fed her anger. My summer vacations would rarely end without a fight of some sort and just like old times, my brother would disappear when the shouting started.

Seeing Mama only once a year allowed me to witness more subtle changes in her. I felt a profound sadness to see her like this—resigned to her life on the island. She had never before let her fears stop her from doing anything. But that was all changing slowly. The hurricane of a woman, the being that could move mountains, the force of nature that was my mother…she was slowly deflating. My little devil was quick to add to the narrative. "She's losing her spark because you left her here alone with your brother. You abandoned her. You don't give a shit about your family."

My sensitivity to other realms was alive and well when I went home on vacations. In the US, it was easy for me to close that door. I was becoming a healthcare professional who believed in "evidence-based practice." If you couldn't prove it, it didn't exist. My schooling had developed my scientific side, which encouraged me to easily dismiss all things spiritual. I was essentially reinforcing my left brain, that hemisphere that deals with all things concrete and finite. Anything I felt out of the ordinary I would always just attribute to my "anxiety disorder," which was the official diagnosis I had been given by my doctor in 2003. Yet, when I went home for the summers, weird things kept happening.

The Azores are said to have powerful energies. Some believe the islands are the location of the lost city of Atlantis. I don't know if that's the case, but my body felt the energies very deeply. In my old bedroom, I became reacquainted with my old guests. But I also had to endure the energies of others. Years later, I would learn that I was an empath, someone capable of taking on someone else's energy and losing theirs to others. Around certain people, I felt very ill. I would be out with friends partying, when someone "dense" would approach me. I called them "dense" because that is exactly what my body felt in their presence. I felt lethargic, exhausted. It was like someone was draining my battery and I couldn't do anything about it. The only way to manage it was to walk away. "Excuse me, but I have to run to the restroom," I'd say when I became overwhelmed. Once back in New York, I would close the spiritual door again and get back to science. Only two people knew of my sensitivities: my mother's sister, Aunt Eva, and my best friend, Jeets. Aunt Eva had been a constant presence in my life since childhood and I trusted her deeply with all issues of my life, especially this one. She understood my sixth sense because she possessed one herself. Our spiritual lineage hadn't stopped at Grandma C. Jeets was also a trusted confidante on all issues of life. We met in 2002 at NYU and were part of the same physical therapy class. I chose to confide in her about my spiritual side not because of our friendship, but because she had an unusual openness to the subject. When I finally got around to telling her that I felt weird things, I was so grateful that she listened with an open mind and heart, which put me at ease.

10 THE NEW YORK YEARS

Life in New York was wonderful. Well, as wonderful as it can be when one lives with a closed heart. I met beautiful friends who still fill my heart with joy. Manhattan is the kind of place where one can easily get lost in entertainment and fun. My classmates and I used to joke about how lucky we were to have made it through the first summer of courses in graduate school because we spent most of our time partying instead of studying. Every night seemed like a great opportunity to explore the endless bars and restaurants the city has to offer. I initially settled in with three classmates in an apartment close to school, in the midtown east neighborhood of Murray Hill. Our lives consisted of socializing, going to class and studying for hours at the nearby coffee shop. I spent so much time there, I came to know most of the people that walked in. My favorite character was the schizophrenic lady who would walk in, order a cup of coffee, sit down at the table next me, position her backpack on the table in front of her, and proceed to have elaborate conversations with the bag. Some days, her bag would be the late President Kennedy, whom she would valiantly try to warn about an impending plot against his life. Other days, former President Clinton would get an earful about his sexual misconduct in the White House. I would stare at her and think, "The only difference between her and me is that I can keep my voices inside my head and she cannot." Through that woman, I saw firsthand what the mind can do and the many worlds it can create.

As the months passed, my body started to exhibit the results of my excessive calorie intake. I just couldn't stay away from three New York City staples: bagels, pizza, and cocktails! Munching on a NYC bagel is like eating a piece of heaven and the pizza was even better than what I had on a trip to Italy as a teenager. And of course, the cocktails are endless. I was committed to exploring my new city—even if that added pounds to my frame.

Great as life was, I still steered clear of romantic entanglements—but not meaningless sex. I avoided relationships because I was terrified of letting anyone close. Marching in step with that was another, even deeper issue: my sexuality. I was having sex with men, but I knew in my heart that I was gay. I could understand why I struggled with the first issue, but the second one puzzled me. After all, I had a loving, supportive family and knew they wouldn't reject me for being gay. But homosexuality would make me even more different than I already felt. I was afraid of being criticized or standing out. Being accepted was a necessity because it helped increase my dismal sense of self-worth. The need for acceptance overrode my growing sense of emptiness. I felt a deep void inside and I was using sex with men as a means to fill it. Yet, with every passing encounter, I felt the void deepen.

As the years passed, I became a real city girl. I loved the Manhattan skyline and the constant buzz of life with 8.4 million other human beings. It was amazing to walk down the street and hear multiple languages, all within just a few blocks. Much as I loved it, however, part of me longed for the presence of nature. My soul always found a way to emerge when I was in nature, but in the Big Apple, I was hemmed in by concrete and skyscrapers. Not even majestic Central Park could sooth my longing, as every inch of the 843-acre park bustled with people, dogs, cyclists and dreamers. Anytime I felt suffocated, I blamed the absence of nature, once again looking outside of myself for the source of my pain. My little devil was hard at work trying to find things in my environment to blame for my discomfort. Years earlier, I had identified the source of my pain, when I stood in my grandma's bathroom holding a bottle of pills. Back then, I knew my suffering was caused by my mind. So what had happened? Why did I again fall into the old pattern of blaming my environment for my pain?

Our egos have an amazing ability to rebuild themselves after a painful life event occurs. When we encounter a situation that hurts us, our minds temporarily lose their power. It suddenly dawns on us—the authentic us—that we have no control over life. Control is an illusion created by the mind. So when something traumatic happens, the mind is exposed for the fraud it has created. We cannot protect ourselves from experiencing pain and sooner or later, we all realize this. In fact, the mind creates more pain if we let it.

What I experienced during those New York years was a common mental phenomenon I call "rebuilding the dams." When a dam breaks, it can cause severe damage downstream: lands can be submerged, economies upended, thousands can die. When something catastrophic happens, the population is quickly reassured that nothing like it will ever occur again. The answer is to build a stronger, more state-of-the-art dam. Take any disaster—from nuclear power plant failure in Japan to levy failure in New Orleans during Hurricane Katrina—and you will find the same response: rebuild stronger structures. The same phenomenon occurs with our psyches. When we experience a painful event, it rocks the very foundation of our mental models. We temporarily see that control is an illusion. And in this delicate but critical time, we have one of two choices. We can decide that we will no longer allow our minds to create models or we let our little devils rebuild the dam.

As hard as it may be to accept, this really is a choice. In fact, this is one of the few areas in your life where you do have complete control. You either choose to live with an open heart—accepting all that comes to you—or you choose to let your mind rebuild the model that gives you a false sense of security. And remember, every time you let your mind rebuild the dam, it will reinforce itself to be stronger. Every painful life event will cause you more and more suffering. We all know this to some extent. Why does our suffering become harder to bear as we age? It's simple. We've allowed our minds to rebuild the dam multiple times over. Each time that dam breaks, it's more excruciating. The good news is, the universe always gives us a chance to change. With every painful life event, there is always the possibility to choose another path. What if we just stopped rebuilding the dams?

11 I KISSED A GIRL

By 2007, my practice as a physical therapist evolved to focus on pediatrics. Working with children warmed my heart and I loved my job—especially my co-workers. To the outside eye, my life was going well. I managed to live somewhat happily, if alone. I was in my late 20s, so the absence of any kind of dating made my friends laugh a bit. "I'm perfectly happy this way," I would reply, with a shrug. It could be completely true. We can all be perfectly happy without being in a relationship. In fact, if you are not already happy with yourself and use someone else to fill that void…that's a real recipe for disaster. My problem was that I wasn't dating because I avoided people out of fear of loss, that dreadful emotion that I carried for so many years. Deep within, I did want to be involved with someone. I wanted to experience the feeling of being "in love." But I just wouldn't admit this to anyone, including myself. My little devil was still in charge and he just kept whispering that I was unlovable.

The wonderful thing about the universe is that you always end up getting what you need, not necessarily what you want. It has this way of sending you "gifts," should you choose to look at them that way. And that is exactly what happened to me when I found myself standing outside a New York City bar one early autumn day, kissing a woman. She was a work colleague and I had sensed a little chemistry before a group of us decided to go out for happy hour drinks. She was attractive, blond and blue-eyed, with a deep sexy voice. After a few drinks, the mutual attraction surfaced. But staying true to my closed heart, I decided not to do anything about it. My mental model was still there, in control. Or so I thought. As we walked out of the bar and stood outside chatting for a bit, she simply kissed me, with no warning or time for me to flee. And as her lips touched mine, I felt that void—a void I had been trying to fill with men—suddenly disappear. She would become the first real relationship I had ever had. I quickly fell in love with her and we dated for almost a year. She was exactly what I needed at that point in my life, even if I wasn't yet prepared to see this truth. Just like me, and most people on this planet, Melanie* had a little devil on her shoulder, too. Her mental model was strong and involved traumatic past experiences that she still carried with her. In retrospect, I was experiencing the Law of Attraction, in which like attracts like. Melanie and I had similar core issues, one of which was fear.

We spent the first few months in love. For the first time in my life, I understood what this feeling was and why our culture focuses on it so much. It does feel blissful, at least for a little while. But along with the blissful feelings, I was still carrying my pain. Plus, my little devil hadn't disappeared. He was alive and well and had worked up a new line of attack. "She's going to leave you," he'd frequently say, "because everyone leaves you." I internalized this message and felt panicked. Melanie was messing up the mental model I had devised as an 18-year-old and this was causing internal commotion. My mental model kept the walls built up high around my heart, but now this person was slowly tearing them down. What was I going to do? My clever mind devised a compromise: I would hang on to her tightly, but only really let her approach the castle walls. She could stand by the gate, but never really enter. This way, I could have the best of both worlds. I'd stay safely hidden behind my walls and I could still partially feel love.

All was good for a little while until the universe sent me more gifts. Melanie was emotionally unstable. She was restless. Her mental model started to clash with mine. The more tightly I held on to her, the more she wanted to escape. I was terrified of losing her, so my grip just kept getting stronger. I gave her everything—affection, attention and adoration but not my heart—because that was all I knew. I had felt worthless for so long and one way I had found to increase self-worth was to constantly please others. Yet my fixes were external. Whenever I encountered a problem in life, the solution was always to manipulate my environment. I always looked outside of myself.

The universe sends you what you need in order to evolve. I knew this on some level since I had become a student of Buddhism. For years, I was a regular at Barnes and Noble, sitting on the floor in the spirituality section, combing through books about Buddha for hours. His life fascinated me and his message had an uncanny resemblance to another spiritual teacher I loved: Jesus. The deepest similarity I found between the two was that the core of their spiritual message rested on inner silence. I had no idea how to silence my chaotic inner world, but I felt a deep longing to be still, to stop hurting. Buddha had been asked once what enlightenment meant. "It is the end of suffering," he responded. Seems relatively simple— stop suffering and you become enlightened. But how the heck does one stop suffering? The answer is both difficult and liberating. Just stop rebuilding the dam. Stop living through your mental model. I didn't have the slightest idea of how to do this, so I just kept moving along with life and listening to my little devil.

As my relationship with Melanie deteriorated, I took a trip to Vancouver and spent some time with family there. When I confessed to my cousin that things were a little rocky in the love department, she insisted I go see her psychic. I laughed outright. I was a member of the medical community and was internally trying to dismiss my connection to other realms. But there was a part of me that knew certain people possessed the ability to communicate with other forms of reality. If I could do it, so could others. And so, I agreed to go to the psychic, because my cousin recommended her. But there would be rules: I would stay silent. If the psychic was a fraud, I wouldn't be coaxed into revealing details of my life.

Trisha* lived in a normal home that looked pretty much like every other house on her block—no pentagrams painted on the garage door, no glitter balls hanging from the trees. But once inside, it was clear this wasn't a regular suburban family home. The walls were decorated with images of Hindu gods and goddesses. There was a strong smell of herbs and incense that assailed my nostrils and stuck to my clothes. I sat in the dining room for a while, waiting. Someone else was with the psychic in the next room, but either the walls were thick or they were speaking softly. When my turn came, Trisha dove right in, with nothing in the way of formalities. After a slight nod and a hello, she began the session by mumbling multiple dates and asking if they meant anything to me. Staying true to my rules, I just answered no. She has to be a fraud, I thought. Suddenly, she looked over at the other side of the room. "There is a man here for you. He's medium build, has salt-and-pepper hair, his hands are very big, and I see smoke coming from behind him. It's like something is burning behind his back. I have no idea what that means."

I sat up straight at attention. I knew it had to be Dad. The smoke part made me laugh out loud. "You know who it is?" she asked. "Yes," I replied. "It's my father." She asked me what was signified by the smoke. I smiled. "Dad was a closet smoker," I said. "He tried very hard to hide his habit." Throughout his life, he knew it infuriated me and my mother because it only added more damage to an already disease-riddled body. He would smoke out in the fields and if I surprised him, he would quickly take his burning cigarette and hide it behind his back. We would both just stand there in silence for a few seconds while smoke curled up from behind his back. I would smile and say, "Dad, I can see you're smoking. There's no point in hiding it." He'd look like a child being scolded for doing something naughty, and it made me laugh every time.

As the psychic talked about Dad, I started to slowly change my mind about her. I hadn't given her any details, but that didn't seem to deter her. "Your father tells me he passed quickly and with no pain. His heart failed him, but he was given a choice in that moment. He tells me he could have stayed on earth, but that his body would not be the same. So he chose to leave. He didn't want to burden his family anymore. He loves you and says he was not alone. His father came to get him. He doesn't want you to feel guilty anymore." Wow. Those few sentences rocked my world. I felt an immediate sense of relief. It had been many years since Dad's death and I had buried all this so deep inside. Yet these revelations brought the pain back to the surface as if everything had happened yesterday.

After a few ruminations about my mother, the psychic changed course. "Your brother will be fine. His fear of flying is leftover trauma from a past life, where he died in a plane crash." I was speechless. My brother Carlos has always been terrified of flying and would have a panic attack at the slightest bump. It struck everyone as odd, since he'd never been on a bad flight. But suddenly, it all made sense. Talking about past lives didn't alarm me either, since I fully believed in reincarnation.

My study of reincarnation had reached beyond Buddhism. Over the years, I wanted to better understand what Grandma C was doing during her cleansing rituals. We are all on different evolutionary paths, I discovered, so some souls linger behind after bodily death. We know them as hauntings and they scare people half to death just like the "guests" in my room terrified me. Trapped souls may appear evil, but they are simply stuck in a realm they know. The more unevolved a soul, the denser they feel to those who can experience their energy. It was this density that Grandma C felt when she did her rituals and it was the same feeling I had around the guests in my room or at nightclubs with friends. Density feels dark and frightening, which is why I tried to close that door so many times. Later, I would learn from personal experience that dense souls cause no harm. They are attracted to light and will go on their way if you help them.

Just as I was digesting the psychic's revelations about my brother, she hit me with more. "This current person you are with. This is going nowhere. Let it go. This person is not for you. Your love will come after. You will travel a lot with him and I see you in Indonesia, on some sort of river boat. What connection do you have to Indonesia? I keep seeing Java, Indonesia." I was so frozen with the first part of what she said that it took me a bit to process her question. My connection to Indonesia? I had none. I had never been there, nor had I ever thought of traveling there. "I have no connection to Indonesia," I responded. She was undeterred. "Well, you will. I can see it." But I caught something she was wrong about. She called my future love a "him," but, I knew I was gay. I didn't say anything—it didn't matter, so I skipped over that and bounced back to her first revelation. "This relationship is pointless?" I asked, devastated. "There is no future there. Let it go," she said, matter-of-factly." But I was in love with Melanie, so by the time I returned to New York, I'd already forgotten what Trisha had said.

The truth has a way of finding you, whether you want it or not. A few weeks after returning from Vancouver, Melanie ended our relationship. She didn't give many reasons, just that she needed a break. My little devil mocked me in my anguish. "Ha! I told you she would leave you!" He was so right. For weeks after that, I was immersed in deep thoughts. I started to think that perhaps it was my karma to lose people in this life. But why?

Karma is often misused in Western cultures. Its true meaning is simply that we plant a seed and later reap the fruit of that seed. But in the West we use karma as if it means fate or destiny, which allows us to remain victims. If you consider yourself a victim, you will continue living your life as it is, without taking full responsibility for everything that happens to you. It means you can continue being passive and not change your mental model. You can just blame life for everything that happens to you. But there is an alternative. You can choose to do the hard work.

I learned about taking responsibility for my actions years later, whilst taking a conflict management class. The professor conducted a simple exercise that involved a repeating scenario. It's 2am and you are sitting at a red light at a particular intersection. Suddenly, you are rear-ended by someone who was not paying attention. Clearly, the accident was not your fault. Our professor asked, "Was it your responsibility?" and we all said no, clearly not. The scenario then repeats. The next day, you are at the same intersection, at the same time. Again, you get rear-ended and again, it is not your fault. The professor again posed his question. This time, only one person in class didn't answer in the negative. "Yes, it is my responsibility," my colleague Sveltana said. "I would change my driving route." After ten rounds of being rear-ended and declaiming the fault, the professor paused and asked another question. "Who has sustained the most damage?" Sure enough, out of all of us, Svetlana had incurred much less damage by taking responsibility and changing course, while the rest of us idiots kept blaming someone else and repeating our behavior. I finally understood the difference between "being at fault" and "taking responsibility."

There are so many events in our lives that are not our fault. If a woman gets attacked on the street, it's clearly not her fault. But she can still take responsibility. How? Let's pretend there are two women, Sandy and Jane. One day, quite separately, they're both mugged. Sandy is so traumatized, she stops walking outside by herself. She lives in a constant state of stress. Jane, too, has been mugged, and as with Sandy, it's not her fault. Wrong place, wrong time. She's also shaken and needs a couple of days to re-center herself. But Jane decides she doesn't want it to change her essence. She's happy and wants to stay that way. She breathes deeply and lets the experience pass right through her. Who suffers more, Sandy or Jane? They both experienced the same event, but one takes responsibility for that which really causes suffering—the inner workings of the mind. There's a quote by Haruki Murakami in his best-selling book, *What I Talk About When I Talk About Running*, that illustrates this truth well. "Pain is inevitable. Suffering is optional."[1] Applying these words to our story means that Sandy and Jane both experienced pain when the mugging took place. There is no doubt all of us will experience painful moments in our lives—even the greatest enlightened spiritual teacher did. But suffering is different. Spiritual teachers often use the word suffering to refer to the mind-generated pain that occurs after an event takes place. In our example, only Sandy suffers, not Jane. Sandy stops walking outside by herself because her mind is telling her things like, "it's dangerous to walk alone," or "you're going to get mugged again and this time it will be worse." She feels paralyzing fear in response to these thoughts. That mind chatter which Sandy acts on is what is creating "suffering". I prefer to call it something different. I like to say that Jane is living with an open heart. She accepts that something painful has happened to her, but she breathes and refuses to listen to what her little devil is whispering.

What does it even mean to live with an open heart? A closed heart resists life. We all know what it feels like to close our hearts to someone who is saying something unpleasant. As they talk, the body tightens. We may clench our jaw, tighten our fists, contract our shoulders, hold our breath and feel a knot in our stomach. Our inner dialogue chips in, too, with "What the hell does he know? This guy's an idiot." Does this sound familiar? You're tightening up your body to resist the unpleasant words and emotions they elicit. But your rigid body will not prevent the person from saying hurtful words. The same truth applies to every unpleasant event in your life. If someone cuts you off, tightening your body does nothing to prevent the event. In fact, it's already happened by the time you clench your jaw. What if you decided to relax instead of contracting? What if you let the unpleasantness pass right through you? What if you decided to let your anger at someone cutting you off process right through your body? Remember Panache Desai's words: "Emotions are energy in motion." The day you let life events—good or bad—pass right through you without contracting or holding on is the day that you begin to live with an open heart.

12 FINDING LOVE

When Melanie left me, I blamed karma. You know how it goes…everyone leaves me, it's just my fate. Poor little Tina. So I closed up again. I clenched my jaw, tightened my body and felt horrible knots form inside my stomach. I was in love with this woman and the only way I was going to let her go was by kicking and screaming. Did my resistance change the fact that she had left me? No. I was fighting that which had already happened. What a waste of energy. Holding on to the past can be truly destructive and I already knew this on a deep level. Although I was completely unconscious to this, I let my past experiences cloud my present. I let my little devil exert power over me.

For months afterwards, I was confused. Melanie had remained at the gates of my heart, so why was I suffering? I didn't yet understand that living with a closed heart doesn't protect you from pain. I didn't yet understand that it may do something altogether different, something deeply wounding. What if I build a castle wall to protect a city from invaders, but then discover that my biggest enemy is already inside? The wall traps my enemy, where he can foment chaos and suffering. Once again, after all these years and a change of life, I corked

64

my bottle of champagne.

By 2009, I needed to meet new people. Maybe my impenetrable heart was speaking to me, maybe it was whispering from the past or perhaps it was Trisha's message finally beating its way into my hard-headed skull. Whatever the influence, I signed up with a dating website. I decided to give the whole dating thing another go. I hadn't changed much. The mental model was there, and so was that little bastard devil. But I figured online dating would be the perfect venue for someone like me. I could go on dates, but if someone was interesting enough to pose a danger to my heart, I could just bid them farewell and reach out to someone else on cyberspace. One day, I received an automated email from the site, with pictures of possible matches. Only one photo caught my attention, a full body image of a woman with flowing blond hair. I had seen this picture before. In fact, months before, I had "winked" at her on the website, but she never answered. Her face truly captured me and I explored her profile in more detail. I nearly laughed out loud. She was from Indonesia. Damn you, Trisha! I was stunned. I perused her profile, reading every word she had written. She was American, but raised in Indonesia and considered that her home. "I'll try the wink again," I thought to myself. "The worst that could happen...she'll think I'm a stalker. Who cares?" I winked. But I felt compelled to say something more this time. I told her a bit about me, that I grew up on an island and loved sports— particularly football, as Europeans call soccer—and music. She responded the next day.

Date received: February 16, 2009
Subject: RE: Hello:)
Hi Tina,

So I have a confession. I read your profile and my first thought was that you had somehow stolen from my "about me" and put it as yours. When I realized that this was, in fact, describing you ... I may or may not have signed up for the "three-day free trial" just to send you a message. Ha! ;)

In short, I'd have to say we have a lot in common. I'm dedicated to fitness (have done two sports to a reasonably high level, and am now trying to find a third), but have also been in the arts for most of my life. I love the theatre (musicals especially), travel, exploring, coffee, and people, of all sorts and shapes.

I also grew up on a little island, but this one in the Pacific – Java, Indonesia – and have since traveled the globe in search of adventure, while trying to make the world a better place. :) I did my doctorate at Oxford (England) in International Development. As disciplines go, I'd call myself something of a political anthropologist, but I really just want to understand how the world works, and what makes people tick. And oh, having lived in England for the past 7 years, I totally understand people obsessed with football (and no, I won't call it soccer ...) ;)

In any case, I will be honest:

You are the first person on here to catch my eye. I think we share a lot of similar interests, and in the least, we'd have fun hanging out! I moved to New York last fall so am still relatively new to town, and keen to meet new and interesting people. So, if you like, drop me an email. I will be discontinuing this "free trial" in about a day or two and no longer able to read messages left here.

Cheers,
Catherine*

My heart was still racing as I reread the message. Could this be the person Trisha mentioned? I was excited... delighted...terrified. But I wrote back that very same day.

02/16/09
Hi Catherine;

I was smiling when I read your email. That's very sweet that you actually did the "free trial" thing to send me a message. :)

I'm really fascinated by your degree and would like to hear more about it. One of my dreams is to travel the world working as a physical therapist. My specialty is pediatrics and I work with children who have severe disabilities. That is something I would like to do overseas also.

My job is very emotionally challenging at times, but I cannot imagine life without my little "peanuts" (as I affectionately like to call them!). They brighten my world every day :) So when I'm having a bad day (usually due to something pretty trivial in the grand scheme of things), all it takes is a smile from a "peanut" to completely change my perspective on life :)

I'm from the Azores...it's ok if you don't know where that is. Very few people know about it. I guess that's why the islands are so untouched and amazingly beautiful. They are a chain of islands that belong to Portugal. I was raised there and go home every year to see my family. My work schedule is conducive to a lot of traveling because I have many weeks of vacation every year. I also choose not to work summers, so life is actually not so bad :)lol

As for sports and exercise, I must confess I've been a little lazy lately. I recently moved and so have been trying to find a gym in my new neighborhood (West Harlem) that has all the stuff I need. My old building had a gym in it so working out was easy for me! The most I've been doing lately is yoga :)

I would love to know more about you! I'm in California on vacation (as I said...I have lots of vacation time!) until Friday. Let me know if you would like to grab a drink or coffee over the weekend.

Nice to hear from you :)
Tina

A few days later, we met at a bar in the East Village. I had gone to my fabulous Latina hairdresser to get ready. I've always had lustrous, dark brown hair, but on this day Maria outdid herself. She'd straightened the natural body to just a wave at the end and it shone brilliantly. I had, as Catherine would later dub it, "Farrah Fawcett hair."

As I got out of the cab at the address noted online for the bar, I couldn't find anything resembling its name. I paced back and forth between 13th and 14th streets for a little while, before asking a stranger if he knew where this particular bar was located. "Oh yeah. Walk into that Chinese restaurant and the bar will be behind a door at the back of the dining area." He rushed off too fast before I could ask, "The bar is at the back of a Chinese restaurant?" Great. "I'm going to have my first date with this hot girl from Indonesia in a sketchy joint at the back of sketchy restaurant. This isn't starting off so well." I walked into the restaurant and perhaps it was because I looked overdressed to be eating cheap Chinese food, one of the waitresses immediately pointed to a door in the back of the room. "Thank you," I whispered. Then I opened the door and there it was: a fantastic trendy bar, equipped with animal print seats and good-looking people everywhere! It was like I had entered another world. "Who the heck ever thought of putting a bar like this behind a dining area smelling of fried egg rolls?"

As I settled in at the bar, I was clearly nervous and excited. Would she like me? My mind raced over the likelihood of finding love online…what was that number again? Shit, I couldn't remember. The bartender brought me a fruity cocktail with a weird name from the extensive menu. I sipped it. Sipped it again. And then, my future wife came into view. She was more beautiful in person than in pictures. Oh my, the depth of her eyes. The old saying that "our eyes are the windows to our souls" certainly applied to Catherine. Her gaze revealed a powerful inner light, as well as some deep-seated pain. After a few drinks and a great conversation, I got up to leave, but something kept me lingering. I had promised a friend I would stop by her house party, but felt weird asking this person I had just met if she wanted to come. One of the many rules in my Dating 101 manual was this: Never take a first date to meet your friends. Yet I didn't want to leave her. So I just put it out there. "I'm going to a friend's party now, but you are welcome to come if you'd like." She smiled. "Well, I'd love to come since I'm not ready to part ways with you yet."

And that was it. Our first date lasted 14 hours and we were inseparable after that. I won't lie: my initial attraction to Catherine went further than her eyes. She was incredibly beautiful and had one of those tight athletic bodies that asked to be explored. And that is exactly what I did. A week later,

Catherine had some friends over. We drank a lot and had a wonderful time. At the end of the night, one of her friends decided to play a joke. Catherine had a meticulously coordinated bookshelf. It was both color and theme coordinated—all to appease her OCD tendencies. Mischievously, the friend switched up all the books on the shelf without her noticing. A few minutes later, she walked by the shelf and was paralyzed with anxiety. I hadn't realized just how important it was for those books to be displayed just so. She then spent the next 45 minutes staring at the bookcase and slowly putting all the books back in order. Since it was 4am, I gently tried to pry her away. "Why don't you come to bed and we can fix that in the morning?" She didn't respond or budge. I knew she would not be able to fall asleep with her books in disarray, so I just sat there watching her. It was at this exact moment that I loved her, wildly, deeply and without barriers. I also finally understood the difference between being "in love" and "loving." The feeling I felt for her was completely different than the one I had felt for my ex-girlfriend. I knew I wanted to spend the rest of my life with her.

The next day, I looked through the books and saw that she had a particular interest in feminism. I sat on the couch next to her with a cup of tea. "Talk to me about feminism," I said. Months later, I asked her if there was a specific time when she knew she loved me. "It was on that day you asked about feminism. In that conversation, I saw how smart and thoughtful you were. You were inquisitive and I loved your thirst for knowledge." Yes, my thirst for knowledge had been alive and well for many years. I considered myself an intellectual—among so many other labels I used to define who I was. I used labels because it gave me an externally derived sense of worth where I was lacking an internal one. There was a part of me that understood this, but my brain just kept overriding it. It seems my soul was trying to tell me something, but I just wasn't listening. My soul was whispering, "Those labels are not who YOU are. You are so much more."

The reason I wasn't listening to my soul was that it had a different language. Our little devils—our egos—speak to us in words and thoughts. That is why it's so easy to listen to that voice in your head since our brains dominate most of our experience. The soul on the other hand, speaks to us through feelings and those are much more complicated to understand—especially if we use our minds to translate them. I literally felt funny whenever I heard Catherine introduce me to her work colleagues. She would always make a point of telling them I had a doctoral degree and was very smart. Hearing her use my labels made me feel uncomfortable, but I never said anything to her. She was just starting out her career at a prestigious global consulting firm and as such, was surrounded by highly cerebral people, so I found myself quickly immersed in a world of Ivy League graduates with accomplished careers, and strangely enough, very low self-esteem. "How could so many highly successful people have such a shitty sense of self-worth?" I'd often wonder. Of course, instead of asking this question of others I could have easily asked it of myself. But it's always easier to look outside.

As our love grew, we began to call each other "beloved." The name just fit perfectly and described well exactly how we felt. We made plans for the future, went on many adventures together and lived happily. Kayaking with crocodiles in the Everglades, touring Bermuda on a moped, hanging out with wonderful friends in Oxford and London, partying away in Lisbon, snorkeling in Cancun, hiking in Sedona. Endless adventures. We had moved in together into a beautiful 28th floor apartment with loads of light and a view of the Hudson River. In this space, we became known for hosting marvelous parties that included endless amounts of booze and wonderful food made by resident chef Tina. I have always had a talent for cooking, courtesy of Mama Idalina and my own love of flavors. Catherine and I were even compatible in the dinner party hosting duties. Since I was the house chef and she couldn't cook an egg, our hosting roles were thus established: I made elaborate dishes, she drank wine and answered the door with a smile. A very fair division of labor indeed. We laughed about this a lot. Laughter…another staple of our relationship in those first years.

But just as my love grew daily, so too did my fear of loss. It was my ball and chain. But what would I do now? With Melanie, I held on to her, but only allowed her to approach my fortress. Catherine was different. I loved her more than I had ever thought possible, for my closed heart. How would I live like this—torn between fear and love? By the time my mind got around to this predicament, my beloved had already torn down the gates and was inside my castle walls. It happened all so quickly and with such intensity that I had no time or strength to put up the normal defenses. It was as if she was my home. And the truth was my love for Catherine was much stronger than the fear. Love was winning. Having lived without love for so many years, I felt like someone who finds an oasis in the middle of a desert.

My panic attacks had quieted down. I was alone for most of them, but I had become proficient at calming down before the heart flutters turned into full blown attacks. Over the years, I had sought counseling. One form, Cognitive Behavioral Therapy or CBT, seemed to work. I remember breaking down my panic attacks into small thoughts and the last one was "fear of death." When the therapist asked, "What is the worst that can happen?" I immediately answered "I die." As I walked home from that session, I started to truly look into this fear of dying. "What if I just fall over right now and die? The world wouldn't end and I believe I would live on. So why am I so afraid of death?" I knew on a deep level that my anxiety over my own demise wasn't shared by the people around me. "Are you afraid of dying?" I once asked Jeets. "No. When it happens it happens. I'm not going to lose sleep over it."

Although I knew my fear of death was out of the ordinary, I

couldn't pinpoint how to change that ingrained thought. So I just continued mastering the art of calming down when the attacks jolted me out of bed at 3am. Yet of late, they returned with a vengeance. I would wake up in the middle of the night in terror, my heart racing fast and my lungs hyperventilating. I was so used to weathering the panic attacks alone that I never once woke up Catherine. I would just quickly jump out of bed and head to the bathroom. Once there, I would slowly regain my ability to think. My heart rate would slow. At times, I'd curl up on the floor, sobbing in grief and fury. I hadn't cried in years and it made me angry that these stupid attacks were squeezing the tears out of me.

Emotions and energy want to move through you. And tears are the best way to do this. Tears literally cleanse your soul of all the grime that has accumulated over it. We all know this to some extent because when we do allow ourselves to cry, we feel immediate relief. Why do you think that is? We feel relief because those tears have unblocked some energy that was stuck inside us. It doesn't matter if we can identify the energy or emotion that was released. What really matters is that we feel so much better. So my question is this: why don't we allow ourselves to cry more often? It's so odd that our society considers dry eyes as a sign of strength. Yet to me, strength is living with a heart open to all the vagaries life throws at us. We choose to close our hearts because we are afraid of being hurt. In essence, we are scared of life. What if we actually looked at a crying grown man and praised him for his strength? I wish we can someday reach this level of evolution.

13 FESTERING WOUNDS

Two years after we started dating, Catherine and I became engaged. We had gone on another adventure, this time to the breathtaking hills of Sedona, Arizona. The place really is magical and I felt bewildered by the red rock shining bright under the sun. We had already decided to get married and had visited a custom jeweler in New York to design our rings. We both disliked the whole "diamonds are forever" culture, so we chose simple stones and settings with wave patterns on them. We wanted our rings to have an ocean theme—representing our island upbringing. What I didn't know was that Catherine wanted to propose to me while we were out hiking, so she had the jeweler expedite the order. Unfortunately, the weather was particularly cold that day so we stayed in the hotel. She quickly moved to Plan B and called me out on the balcony of our room, overlooking the red hills. We stood on the balcony in silence for a few seconds before she started talking. "You know, I have loved you since we first met...." I interrupted her midway through the sentence to crack a joke. "That's not true!" She looked at me, irritated. "Shut up! I'm trying to tell you something!" It was then that I realized she was going to propose. She was shaking and visibly nervous. She looked beautiful in that awkwardness. When she asked me to marry her and I said yes, it immediately started snowing. I looked at the hills and stuck my hand out to catch some snowflakes. It was all just perfect. In my excitement I said, "It's snowing in the desert! Just like this snow in the desert, we, too, are different. But God loves us just the same."

Although I still never said a word to Catherine, my fear had reached terrifying levels. As so many times before, I desperately searched for solutions outside of myself to soothe the pain. I thought I could stop hurting by changing my environment. I became more materialistic—as if a new piece of furniture or a handmade Italian bag could somehow bring me inner peace. I also started to rely more heavily on my intellectual label. I devoured books on political theory and economics. I wanted to always know more about a specific topic than anyone else in the room. But worse than that, I continued believing the myth that the cause of my suffering was outside of me—either in the form of a person or thing. I continued to hold on to my battered old mental model and to view my world with "old eyes." What does it mean to live with "old eyes?" It means we react to life's events by consistently relying upon past experiences to form our responses. Yet, the past is long gone. Life is a creative process. The universe is constantly expanding and there are a billion different events during a lifetime that can color your viewpoint. And here is the hardest part to accept: you have absolutely no control over what comes at you. Not only that, but our brain stores only a small fraction of what happens to us, particularly the most traumatic parts.

Dr. Elizabeth Kensinger— a psychologist at Boston College—conducted a review of evidence on memory and found some interesting results.

> "The results just described point to a role for negative emotion in boosting not only the subjective vividness of a memory but also the likelihood that event details are

remembered. Although it would be simple to conclude from these studies that any emotional experience is likely to be remembered with additional detail, the story may not be so straightforward. The valence of an event (i.e., whether it is pleasurable or aversive) seems to be a critical determinant of the accuracy with which the event is remembered, with negative events being remembered in greater detail than positive ones." [2]

Scientists are not sure why our brains store painful events more readily than happy ones, but some hypothesize that there is an evolutionary reason for this. Matt Wilson, professor of neurobiology at MIT noted that, "in terms of brain activity, anticipating the future and remembering the past seem to be related. The speculation is that we process memory in order to solve problems. And things we should learn from, things that are particularly important or that have strong emotions tied to them, may be things that are going to be important in the future."[3]

From an evolutionary standpoint, this makes sense. If I were a hunter/gatherer and was attacked by a lion one day, I would remember that event forever! I would also make sure to be extra careful and stay away from anything resembling a lion. This behavior would ensure my survival and the propagation of my genes. So in essence, when you rely upon your "old eyes" to react to the present moment, you are essentially relying upon all your painful experiences. Does that seem like a good way of living each situation that comes your way?

Although most people think human memory works like a digital camera, recording events that remain unaltered in a little storage space in the brain, the truth is a little more complex. In an article in *Wired* magazine, journalist Jonah Lehrer says that "every memory begins as a changed set of connections among cells in the brain. If you happen to remember this moment— the content of this sentence—it's because a network of neurons has been altered, woven more tightly together within a vast electrical fabric. This linkage is literal: For a memory to exist, these scattered cells must become more sensitive to the activity of the others, so that if one cell fires, the rest of the circuit lights up as well."[4]

It's a brilliantly efficient strategy: memories live in various regions of my brain, according to the type of information stored. Storing bits of information in various locations insures I can hold exponentially more stuff inside my brain than the memory of a camera can. But here is the coolest part: our memories are alive, because the neural networks that maintain our memories are delicately altered every single time we recall an event from the past and are based on how we feel in the present. Scientists call this process "reconsolidation." Lehrer continues.

"To be more specific: I can recall vividly the party for my eighth birthday. I can almost taste the Baskin-Robbins ice cream cake and summon the thrill of tearing wrapping paper off boxes of Legos. This memory is embedded deep in my brain as a circuit of connected cells that I will likely have forever. Yet the science of reconsolidation suggests that the memory is less stable and trustworthy than it appears. Whenever I remember the party, I re-create the memory and alter its map of neural connections. Some details are reinforced—my current hunger makes me focus on the ice cream—while others get erased, like the face of a friend whose name I can no longer conjure. The memory is less like a movie, a permanent emulsion of chemicals on celluloid, and more like a play—subtly different each time it's performed. In my brain, a network of cells is constantly being reconsolidated, rewritten, remade. That two-letter prefix changes everything."

The science of memory reinforces many spiritual teachings, especially those with a meditation tradition. If I can't accurately rely on my own memories, what am I left with? If my memories really do change every single time I remember them, then is it really smart to live life by relying on the past or an illusion of the past? This is why disidentification, or removing yourself from identification with your thoughts and mind, is a major teaching in many spiritual traditions. When you admit that your memories of events are not constant and true, you become more flexible, less self-righteous, more accepting of change. If memories change, then so does everything else. So in essence, when you rely upon "old eyes" to react to the present moment, you are relying upon all your painful experiences. Does that seem like a good way of living each situation that comes your way?

Each of life's events is new because it has never actually happened to you. The present moment—this very moment that you read these lines—has never happened in your life. So why not look at the events that come to us with "new eyes?" New eyes recognize that the present moment is always new. New eyes understand that our lives are not like a playlist we put on repeat. Each experience is fresh. Once we recognize this, we start to doubt whether it is prudent to live each moment only through the lens of our memories. That was my little devil: a whole storage file of painful past experiences. And I believed what he said because the message was old, familiar and therefore comfortable. So many of us choose what is familiar, even when it hurts us deeply. I was stuck in the revolving door, using painful old experiences to dictate my present behavior. Where did that get me? I felt more fear, but I was also unable to see my beloved for who she was. My awareness had focused intently on the parts of my fiancée that caused most fear in me. This is one of the reasons why we should cease to live our lives based on the past.

Let's say you are sitting peacefully in the park and someone walks behind you and sounds a horn. Naturally, you turn your head to locate the source. The same applies to any other sense.

Your eyes tend to focus on that which looks "out of place" and disrupts the steady pattern of your surroundings; your tongue will find the most miniscule roughness on your teeth. That is how our senses capture the world. But how does our brain interpret incoming information? If we live unconsciously—without realizing we are not the thoughts in our heads—we focus our awareness on things that cause internal discomfort. We interact with the world based on our responses to learned pain. I carried my pain stored in the filing cabinet of my brain and used it to interpret incoming information. Memories and feeling developed in reaction to past events partly form who we are for the better. But they are a sea anchor on our souls, particularly when those feelings are loneliness, loss, feeling unworthy of love. Of the thousands of pieces of information that my senses captured every day, my awareness would focus only on the ones that poked my learned pain. I walked around with an open wound, focusing only on the things that bumped into it because those were the ones that caused most pain. That meant I would only be bothered by situations that would target my wound. I would start to get upset if Catherine didn't devote enough attention to me, because it poked my fear of loss and sense of worthlessness. As the blister opened, my little devil would soon follow with a whisper, "You're not good enough for her."

So here's an interesting question: Why do we keep picking at those wounds, letting them fester and infect our behavior? It hardly seems worth the effort, and yet, I kept steadily on the cycle of creating the blister and letting it fester. We focus on that which lies outside of us instead of looking within. For me, I protected my wound by getting into arguments with my beloved. I demanded that she pay more attention to me, flirt less, behave a certain way. All these "solutions" were in my environment. I reasoned that her actions caused my pain. Her actions were like razors scraping my wounds. So I wrapped myself in emotional bandages, cocooning my heart from pain. Put like that, it seems reasonable, if a bit naïve and immature.

But what if, instead of dictating Catherine's behavior, I had exposed my wounds to heal. I would no longer have to worry about manipulating my environment in order to stay clear of razors.

And yet....and yet....protecting yourself from emotional pain doesn't work. There are too many variables, too many possibilities in every moment of every day to rationally avoid all pain. It would be like hailing a cab on a busy New York City street. You are simply trying to get a ride, but in the millions of microseconds around that simple act, someone may bump into you, another person may spill his coffee all over your shirt, or you might twist an ankle and fall. In the same way, countless little slices of pain can infect your wound, if you choose to let them. Accept that you cannot control what life sends. Give up the illusion of control. You will realize how much stress, fear, and panic it causes when you ask your brain to protect your wounds from all possible events. Why not choose to heal the wounds? Let them heal.

14 WHEN THE MIND COMMANDS

Shortly after Catherine and I became engaged, I developed an itch. I wanted to change careers, but had no idea where to start. My soul was knocking, but I refused to open the door. When I began to feel a deep call to do something else with my life, my mind was quick to judge. I was good at what I did, I made a comfortable living and had spent years in school training to be a physical therapist. Why on earth would I want to do something else? And just as I would begin to listen to my soul, I would encounter an event at work that would cause my mind to further judge. A parent would approach me and thank me for the work I did with their child. It was wonderful to hear these compliments, but it also tore me up inside. My work involved helping children with disabilities to function better, which was highly rewarding to me. But my soul was singing another song. Without noticing, I was becoming more left brain dominant with each passing day. I sought out more intellectual endeavors, devoured books on a huge range of highly involved topics and began to write about politics. But rather than succor my soul, I was filling my life with outside values in an attempt to define my worth. I needed new labels to counter my feelings of worthlessness. So like a lot of people with an opinion and a keyboard, I became a blogger. I wrote about everything from politics to feminism. I also began to focus my attention on issues about freedom and quickly found a home in the libertarian movement.

A libertarian believes in the ultimate freedom of the individual, the freedom to make choices without outside influence, especially from the government. The idea of ultimate freedom fascinated me, but I was looking for it in all the wrong places. When I began to write about politics, I focused on a false sense of freedom. I was too busy looking outside again. I wrote about freedom from government, freedom from others, freedom from being randomly frisked by police or forced to pass through an X-Ray machine at the airport. Interestingly, although I felt a strong attraction to the idea of freedom, I was only scratching the surface of that which I yearned. It would take a couple more years for me to understand what freedom really meant.

While I was busy writing about external freedoms, my soul remained trapped. I was a prisoner held captive by my own mind. I mused about freedom, while remaining completely ignorant of my own prison. I kept talking about freedom as if I were an expert on the subject but then refused to acknowledge the jail cell I had chosen to live in most of my life. My life was like the movie, The Matrix: I lived one life based on my belief in freedom, but I was a prisoner of a construct I couldn't see or even honestly acknowledge. As my career dissatisfaction increased, so did my sense of worthlessness. I became more self-critical with each passing day. That same self-loathing I felt when my father had died returned. Then again, it probably had never really left.

The year 2010 was an ebb mark in my low self-esteem. Looking back, the fact that so many of us don't like ourselves is puzzling. Why do we find it so much easier to list our faults rather than our excellent attributes? Why do we find it so hard to say thank you to a compliment, rather than dismiss it with a self-deprecating remark? Write down things you dislike about yourself. Is it because your nose is too long, your breasts are too small, you don't make enough money, your car is old, you have thin hair or you have no friends at work? They're all external judgments we and the rest of the world hold up as qualities we should or shouldn't have. Yet the internal qualities—she's a good person, he's generous to a fault—often automatically send up a red flag in our minds, suggesting that those sterling qualities mask other faults. In that way, we use our environment in opposing ways, sometimes to increase our sense of self-worth and sometimes to tear it down.

How odd, don't you think? How can the same physical environment cause completely opposite feelings inside of us? This can only happen when we choose to live with a chaotic internal world. Yes, it is a choice, albeit a painful one to live. Why is our internal world so chaotic? The answer is simple. We refuse to look at it. Every day, we go about living in our mental models, immersed in the dramas we create that really are of no importance, all things considered. While we are distracted, we lose the opportunity for real growth. We lose the chance to calm the chaos inside. We forgo the chance of a lifetime, to center ourselves within and let life unfold naturally. When we learn to be centered, the world changes completely, the chaos ceases to exist. But all of that is easy for me to say. And it's easier to read than to live. At least it was for me.

What does it even mean to center yourself? It means recognizing that you are the watcher of thought, not thought itself. When French philosopher and mathematician Rene Descartes said, "Je pense, donc je suis" or "I think, therefore I am," he was expressing that even the act of doubt proves our existence. But we can take Descartes's philosophical proposition one step further. "I think, therefore I am" can also be referring to the little devil on our shoulders, the ego. The ego is certainly a part of us—an important part—but it is not what defines "I am." Someone who is brain dead, lying in a hospital bed, still exists. The master yogi who can stop all thoughts while in a meditative trance still exists, he still "is." What lies beyond thought is who you really are. You are essentially consciousness, a soul in a body. Think of it like a snail that uses his shell to live. Our bodies, including the brain where thoughts reside, are our shells. We use them while we live on this planet and then discard them once we are done.

When you start thinking of your body as a shell, you realize you are not your thoughts. Thoughts happen. They form in our brains. When you realize that YOU are the soul that watches thought, you are free. Suddenly it dawns on you that the little devil on your shoulder need not be taken seriously. He will never stop talking because the brain always thinks, but you don't need to follow his advice. You can simply say, "Thank you for your opinion," and move on with your day. That is the real definition of freedom…knowing that you don't have to follow your little devil's advice or even believe one word he says. Freedom! It's that simple.

Despite the fact that my beloved and I poked each other's wounds, we were deeply in love. Catherine travelled a lot for her job, but we worked out a way to manage. One strategy was to write love notes to each other in a shared journal. Each letter she left me before she traveled temporarily soothed and reassured my fearful heart, at least for a while.

March 20th, 2011
Beloved,
Another Monday, another flight away from you. At least I know I get to come home to you, which makes me so happy. Yesterday I was very affectionate. I think I started to get worried about work, the future, everything. And then I realized I didn't have to face it alone. You are my home and my future. We will always figure it out together, no matter what. And that brings me peace, and hope, and a deep content I'm not sure I've ever experienced before.
I love you, Tina. With all of my heart, for all of my life. C.

15 WHEN THE SOUL TALKS TO CLOSED EARS

In 2011, we moved to Washington, DC. It seemed like a great idea at the time. She wanted to leave New York and I wanted to change careers, so DC presented us with new possibilities. As we left Manhattan on a warm summer day, I kept looking at the rear view mirror to catch a glimpse of my home's skyline. I had lived in that city for almost ten years and leaving it along with my community and the deep friendships I had made was deeply painful. I am an introvert with extrovert tendencies, which means I live out loud, but my true circle of friends is small and I keep them forever. I cherish my friends as I do my family. My fiancée, on the other hand, was extremely outgoing and made friends easy. She was a real nomad, used to moving through the world at the drop of a hat and at top speed. Leaving New York was an exciting new chapter for her, but she sensed my sorrow and tried to reassure me. "This will be great, Tina. We're going on another adventure together! Everything will be okay."

We settled in a beautiful apartment with a view of the Capitol Building. I looked at it in awe and daydreamed. "That is where all the important political events happen in our country. Maybe I could work there someday!" Yet, they were less goals than passing fancies and never really stirred excitement in me. Since the soul speaks in feelings, I should've seen this as a red flag. Working in politics was a 'good on paper' idea. But it wasn't what my soul wanted.

While I searched for meaning and contentment in the endlessly shifting, often duplicitous world of politics, I found something that did tug at my heart. Shortly after moving to Washington, I traveled to Peru on a mission with Health Volunteers Overseas. I was tasked with providing continuing education to medical professionals in Lima and Cuzco. I had been working with the organization for a while now, having completed another mission to India, in 2010. My students were mostly physical and occupational therapists and my job was to improve their knowledge and skills in pediatrics. I loved every minute of it. Teaching others meant learning for me, too. I was still the sponge I had been as a little girl, looking to be filled with knowledge. And I loved interacting with others people and learning about their cultures. The world, I discovered, was less of our American melting pot and more of what Canadians call "a cultural mosaic."

My soul was talking to me through wonderful feelings of contentment and excitement. We all know what this feels like—to have this surge of emotion that emanates like a glow outwards to our skin. I like to use the world contentment more than happiness. Happiness, to me, is a superficial feeling. Buying a new car can make us happy. Making a lot of money can make us happy. Losing 20lbs, getting Botox to ease wrinkles or being admired can make us happy. It's all about external circumstances. Contentment is a whole other thing. Contentment is the feeling you get when you look at your grandchildren play in the backyard. It's what happens when you wake up next to your beloved, filled with joy. It's the feeling of knowing that, no matter what you personally have contributed to the world, you are living in a state of grace because you have more than you could ever have asked for. You feel contentment and gratitude rise from the bottom of your stomach until it reaches your heart and makes it almost explode with joy. You may crack a smile when you feel it, or laugh out loud, or cry. That is how deep and powerful it is. When you feel emotions surge like this—with this type of intensity—you should listen to them. Your soul is trying to tell you something.

It is important to realize that there is a difference between emotions emanating from the soul and those emanating from the mind. In my experience, soul-centered emotions are those which come before thought arises. You can be gardening and lift your eyes for just a moment to observe where your children are. You see them playing happily and at that moment it you are overwhelmed with love. Soul-centered emotions emanate from love. Mind-generated emotions can be both positive and negative. I don't think they're good or bad, because judging them this way can backfire. It did on me. One of the reasons I had stockpiled so many emotions was because I judged them as bad and didn't want anyone to see that side of me. Anger, rage, fear...they were all labeled negative and kept out of sight from others. I thought that feeling bad emotions was a sign that, I too, was bad. I thought my emotions defined me. But they never do. They are just energy. Energy that needs to pass through you.

So here's a life lesson, me to you. If you feel anger, let it out. If you feel fear, let it out. I'm not talking about acting violently or saying horrible things to someone. In fact, when we restrain and swallow these emotions, we erupt in frustration that expresses itself in violence and shouting. There are times in almost everyone's life when inexplicable frustration and rage well up over the most mundane and pedestrian moments. Perhaps the roast is overcooked. Maybe chores were left undone. Who knows? Suddenly, you are shouting in frustration. Why? You have enough accumulated anger that one incursion becomes the tipping point. Had you let anger pass through you when you initially felt it, had you calmly expressed dissatisfaction in a way that respects the other's autonomy, the argument would never have occurred. It really is that simple. When you feel that rage, breathe deeply and relax your body. Literally feel your body melting like candle wax under a flame.

The same goes for positive emotions, which are also "energy in motion." Let them pass through you. Don't hold on. This one may be more difficult to understand because we all want to hold on to emotions that make us feel good. You're lying in bed in the morning with your beloved. Your beloved looks amazing in the morning light, sleeping peacefully. You realize how happy you are together. Of course, you want to hold on to that moment as long as possible. You want time to stop. But you don't have to keep an iron grip on positive emotions, because the more you learn to let them flow through you, the more you open up space for the soul-centered emotions to make a home within you. When you learn to let energy flow through you, you will find yourself in a constant state of joy. You will find that you don't need to hold on to the emotion you felt while watching your partner sleep because you can feel it every minute of every day. Think of it like a flowing river. You don't need to tightly hold on to a little bit of the water because the stream is never ending. Instead of taking a cup full of water from the river, you can just bring your mouth to the stream and drink indefinitely.

Another thing to remember about mind-generated emotions is that they are usually preceded by thought. You're walking down the street after just having an argument and your mind is busy rehashing the whole episode. As you relive the argument, you notice your anger is getting worse. How is it possible that you feel more anger now, long after the argument, than you did at the time? It's because your thoughts generate more emotions. Your little devil has just coaxed you into increasing your own blood pressure or making your heart race. That's how powerful your mind is. What if you had just breathed deeply three times—that is scientifically guaranteed to lower blood pressure—and relaxed your body just as your co-worker was saying something unpleasant to you? And what if you followed that up with looking at the episode as an expression of their unhappiness and insecurity, rather than a judgment on you? You probably wouldn't be walking down the street rehashing the whole episode. Your blood pressure would have stayed normal and your heart rate slow. This really is a choice.

Yes, my soul was singing when I went to Peru. I just wasn't ready to listen. When I returned to DC, life went back to normal. We planned our wedding, unpacked from the move and tried to navigate our new community. I was also busy reinforcing my left brain, immersing myself in politics and writing for a political website. Yet the more I wrote and knew about politics, the more dead inside I felt. The political environment in DC and throughout the country was toxic and I began to feel disgusted. Politics may be the perfect line of work for some people, but it was certainly not for me. Each political conversation I had drained me. I loved debates and lively conversations, but my soul felt adrift and kept telling me that I would need to let go of my intellectual label, because it was deadening me. I wish I had listened to the rumblings. We all should. When you are doing something that causes you discomfort, it is most likely your soul speaking. I know it can seem like a monumental task to sit quietly and observe your inner world. Eventually, you will be forced to do it. Who will force you? Life. You can try to live by putting your mind in command, but sooner or later, the mind loses. Sooner or later, something will happen that literally forces you to sit down, close your eyes and look inside. This may happen in your teens, your twenties, during a midlife crisis, in your retirement years, or when you are standing at the doorstep of death. When do you want your soul's wake-up call to come? Do you really want to be close to death before you realize that you have spent your whole life living in dramas created by your mind?

The summer of 2011 was absolutely magical, despite my inner turmoil. Keeping to our adventurous nature, we decided at the last minute to get married in New York City before our "real" wedding took place in the Azores. New York State had just passed a marriage equality bill, so I could get married in the city I loved. We exchanged our first vows in Central Park, surrounded by a small group of friends. The ceremony was simple and beautiful. Catherine and some of our friends cried, yet I remained tearless. I cry whenever I recall the day that brought so much joy to my heart. I was exploding with love for my wife. But I was still stuck in the old way of doing things. I was employing the mental model of that scared little girl I used to be. My default was still to bury things deeply within. Even joy, love, happiness. Stoicism. I was ice cold. That was still me. It hurt me deeply to remain closed like this. But I didn't know how to open up. I felt like a 100 meter sprinter who was being asked to perform the high jump. How does an expert in one thing suddenly do another? I needed to practice, but I had no idea where to start. So I kept choosing what was familiar. I was still living life with my "old eyes", which wouldn't even let me shed a tear for the love I felt on that day. Eleanor Roosevelt once put it this way: "We are afraid to care too much, for fear that the other person doesn't care at all."

16 ANOTHER LOSS

The wedding out of the way, things moved so quickly back in Washington that I was getting panicked. I hadn't found a job and the financial burden of a one income family was weighing heavily on my wife. The universe had brought her to me, this wonderful woman so much like me in fundamental ways. We had many of the same issues from fear to panic, from feelings of loneliness and to childhood trauma. It's no surprise that 'like attracts like' is a universal rule. After all, it is easier to look at someone else's issues than it is to examine at one's own. Yet I wasn't just observing my wife's fears. I was also looking in the mirror. She was my mirror. The universe was giving me a gift. Since I hadn't been able to look within and heal myself, the cosmos sent me an external experience to help cure me. A couple of years later, I would stand in our kitchen and tell her that "there is no greater love than to be your beloved's mirror." By then, I understood. But in the summer of 2011, I was still busy looking at my wife's issues as an irritation. It irritated me that she demanded so much of my attention. She seemed too needy. Truth was, I was slowly starving her of affection because I was closing my heart more and more each day. It was the only way I knew how to deal with my fear of loss and ever increasing love I felt for her. But by closing myself, I was inadvertently poking at her fear of rejection. Ironically, we were both acting as mirrors so that we could observe the things in us we needed to change. Yet, we both decided to see with our old eyes and continue using the mental models of who we were as little girls to interact with the world.

Around that time, I consulted with my trusted psychic, Karen. It didn't matter how left brain dominant I became or how many degrees I accumulated, my door to other realms never fully closed. I had become a closeted spiritualist. I wasn't in the closet when it came to my sexuality, but I certainly was when it pertained to my spiritual beliefs. My wife was not only a left brain dominant consultant, she also came from a missionary evangelical family. When we had first met, I tried to talk about my sensitivities to other realms. On multiple occasions I attempted to let her in on my little secret. But every time I approached the subject, she would reply, "I've always been taught that those powers can be evil." It made me feel that, like the healing women burned as witches in Salem hundreds of years ago, I couldn't talk about anything spiritual that would clash with my wife's Christian upbringing. She just wasn't open to it, so I eventually stopped. It was so fascinating to me that a woman who believed in God was nonetheless skeptical about other areas of spirituality. I would have understood this reaction had I been talking to an atheist, but my wife had always been deeply spiritual, albeit not my kind of spiritual. I was resentful of her rigidity. Her rejection of my belief system felt like a rejection of me. Suddenly, I felt more alone than I had before, except for the "visitors" who came every once in a while. Naturally, I never told her about them.

When I got on the phone with Karen, I felt instant relief. It was like I was talking to a sister. I had first met her through my aunts, who visited Karen regularly. Her voice had always soothed me, but her advice was what I really cherished. Just like Trisha, Karen was also gifted. And in the summer of 2011, she was a little more forceful than usual. "The work that you have done up until now on Mother Earth has been most appreciated and needed. But it is time to move on now. Your soul wants to do something else. I see you at a university, surrounded by white coats with a blue logo on them, but I can't read it. Something related to medicine or in an area where medicine is practiced. Your wedding will be beautiful and the surroundings breathtaking. An island wedding, I like it! You two love each other deeply. Your beloved grandmother is here. She is very excited about the wedding. She tells me she believed certain things while on earth. But she says she feels much differently now." I was so happy to hear those words about Vó. She had passed away the year before and her loss was agonizing to me. She died at 99, a devout Catholic. Between her age and her religious beliefs, I never told her about Catherine. I was afraid of her reaction. I loved Vó deeply and didn't want her to judge me.

Talking about Vó with Karen brought some painful recent memories back. My paternal grandmother had stayed true to her nature as a trailblazer up until the day she died. She was still cooking Thanksgiving dinner well into her 90's, had a sharp, agile mind and a forceful nature that didn't brook dissent. So when she laid out exactly what she wanted for her death, it came to no surprise to us all. She made clear that her life not be prolonged by any means, not even the use of an IV drip. Vó wanted absolutely nothing done to artificially sustain her body on this earth. Yet, when the time came to actually follow through on her wishes, it was the most excruciating experience of my life.

One day, Vó had a stroke that left her right side paralyzed. When she returned home, she was just not the same. She was ready to leave and we could all tell. When she had a second stroke, the doctors said there was nothing left to do. She wanted to die at home so my family promptly made arrangements to accommodate her. I flew to California and arrived just as Vó's ambulance pulled up the driveway. When they brought her in and gently lay her on the medical bed my family had obtained, she was unconscious. As hope that I would speak to her again faded, she opened her eyes and immediately recognized me. I cried, ran my fingers through her hair and kissed her wrinkled face. For years we had called her our *ovelhinha*, Portuguese for 'little sheep.' It was an endearing name we came up with because Vó kept her snowy white hair always meticulously fashioned in a tight short perm.

She was awake long enough to kiss me multiple times and say "I love you" in broken English. And then she slipped into unconsciousness again. We stayed at her bedside constantly. She would never be alone. We knew Vó probably wanted to die alone, but none of us could bear leaving the room. The next day, as I sat next to her and massaged her paralyzed arm, she awoke. She was thirsty. In fact, she was slowly dying of dehydration. It's amazing to me how our bodies can override our wills in these times. Vó had made us promise: no artificial means including IV fluids. Yet here she was—her body desperately seeking water. "*Água*", she whispered in my ear. We ran to the kitchen to grab water, but knew she wouldn't be able to drink from a cup. Her throat muscles had been damaged by the stroke and she couldn't swallow very well. We filled a sponge with water and slowly gave it to her. She sucked the sponge dry and asked for more. I couldn't bear it. I now understood how difficult it was for family members to comply with medical directives and the wishes of their dying loved ones. It was just excruciating to watch her body wither away. Mercifully, Vó would soon lose consciousness again, this time never to regain it. Vó died alone one week after my visit. Someone had always been by her bedside every minute of every day, but on this day, my godmother Mimi walked over to the dining room for some lunch and when she returned, Vó was gone. My grandmother literally waited to be alone before passing. That was my Vó.

When I returned home to Washington, my heart felt like

exploding. I had lost one of the foundational figures in my life. Yet, the moment I walked through my front door, I dried my eyes and closed my heart again. I have no idea why I didn't want my wife to see my pain. It actually sounds crazy as I write these words, because there is no plausible explanation for anyone to keep this kind of pain from their spouses, but it made sense to my mental model. I had endured loss before and did it alone. Again, I was back to doing things the way I always had, even if it killed me inside. I remember Catherine hugging me and I felt tightness come over my body, because it was the only way I could keep that pain inside. What a sad existence I chose to live. But as if to lessen my pain, Vó would come to visit me a few days later in my dreams. It was one of those dreams you just know is a vision. She looked so happy, laughing out loud while sitting at a table surrounded by other souls. I could see that smile so clearly. Vó was finally at peace and that knowledge made my heart ache a little less.

17 MARRIED ON THE ISLAND

On August 20th, 2011, my wife and I restated our vows on my beautiful island of São Jorge. The whole trip was magical, filled with family, close friends and many sun-filled ocean days. We exchanged our promises on a balcony overlooking the slice of Atlantic Ocean I had gazed upon every day as a girl. That ocean had taught me so much and now it was blessing the most important day of my life. It dawned on me how those waters had witnessed the most significant events in my life, from the first winter in São Jorge to the death of my cousin and father. With each traumatic event, I looked out at my beloved Atlantic and talked to it. Actually, I think those waters were the only real confidante I ever had. They knew every detail about the good and bad moments in my life, they knew who I was at the deepest level and at times they reminded me of what my inner world looked like. The North Atlantic during a storm was a perfect representation of my inner world. Yet on this day, the ocean was calm and sparkling blue under the sunlight.

I was also fully aware of the importance of my wedding on the island community. Our marriage was only the second same-sex union to take place on the island since Portugal had passed a gay marriage bill. Prior to arriving on the island, I was nervous and afraid of being judged by my island community. I was certain that someone would approach me on the street one day and tell me how wrong gay marriage was and that I was going to hell. Yet again, I was living my life through the prism of my mind. In reality, my mind was wrong and just as I was fearful of the judgments of others, I was ignorant to the fact that I, too, was judging them before they judged me. My fears were unfounded. My friends and neighbors were endlessly kind. Nearly 30 people had flown in from various parts of the world to celebrate with us and that meant we needed lots of food. Every day, someone from the island would bless us with gifts that were simple, but thoughtful: eggs, tomatoes, cheese, and bread. Others helped organize our wedding ceremony and decorations. They opened their hearts to us. Our guests were treated wonderfully and I felt such a deep gratitude that my own heart was overflowing.

This episode really illustrated to me how our assessment of others sometimes has nothing to do with them but rather, everything to do with us. Each one of us views others based on our mental models. We not only judge based on our pain, but we also choose to see other people's mental models instead of their souls. When you judge someone else negatively, you make your conclusions based on two things. First, the person poked one of your wounds in some way, maybe by saying something that reminded you of a painful past experience. Second, you fell into the trap of equating them with their mental model. Yet, we already know that we are not our thoughts, but merely the witness of those thoughts. In the end, if someone upsets you, you can decide to judge them or you can instead have a deep recognition that the little devil on their shoulders was directing the offense.

Aware and awake—that's what we can all achieve. It's being able to see that what someone says comes from their past pain, their past joy, from their mental models. The spiritual teacher

Anthony de Mello once said that "no one sins in awareness," meaning that the person who said something hurtful to you was not aware that he or she was not the mind. They were ignorant to the fact that they are the watcher of thought. They were so fully immersed in thought and in using their mental models that they hurt you without wanting to. You might not agree with this statement. You might be thinking "that person hurt me on purpose." But sit a moment in silence and remove yourself from the dramas of your mind. When you are able to sit back in the seat of awareness—watching your mind think without becoming involved in its drama—you will see something beautiful. You will be able to clearly distinguish between another person's soul and their mind.

One soul never wants to hurt another. The soul is pure love and infinite consciousness. It is that simple. It's the mind that gets in the way. It's the mind that formulates and pronounces hurtful things. It's the mind that propels someone to physically hurt another. In essence, someone who is fully aware is incapable of hurting anyone—the soul just does not allow it. Yet there is another important aspect to this all that begs mentioning. No one hurts you unless you allow it. In her book, *This Is My Story*, Eleanor Roosevelt put it this way: "No one can make you feel inferior without your consent."[5]

No two people react in the same way to the same situation. If someone yells and calls me names, I may call them names back. But another person, when faced with the same profanity, might choose to breathe deeply and walk away without saying a word. How is it possible that two people who live the same experience respond so differently? Well, it all goes back to the mental models. If my mental model is one that is built upon worthlessness, then demeaning words will poke my wound and I will feel deep discomfort. Another person may have a strong sense of self and thus is not at all perturbed by someone calling him names. He or she may have entirely different wounds that may be poked by other situations, but worthlessness is not one of them.

We can only be hurt by someone else if we allow it. In essence, we can only be hurt if we choose to live with festering wounds. And we can choose to heal them. Can you imagine the day we all take full responsibility for healing all our wounds? Do you know what would happen if we took on this challenge? We would respond to every event in life with "new eyes" and the lightness of living without baggage. We would be free.

18 IGNORING MY SOUL

When we returned to Washington after our island wedding, my heart was filled with joy. But before long, my little devil was whispering again and I would continue to listen to his every word. After the whirlwind summer we had, my wife and I settled back into normal life. By this time, I had completely decided to change careers. Practicing full time in pediatrics was something I had finally sensed was not in my future. I longed for something different, for a development in my path. At this critical stage, there was a part of me that was finally listening to the rumblings within. Unfortunately, I turned my career change decision into a 'problem' the mind had to fix.

My wife was progressing in her consulting career and I felt deep pride in her journey. However, I felt not only rumblings in me, but also in her. Her job had given her extraordinary skills and the company name meant she would be able to work wherever she wanted. But I sensed she was unhappy. We were both so left-brain dominant that we had allowed our minds to harden us. This phenomenon of left brain dominance is surprisingly common in the West because everything is tailored to fit it. And although the left hemisphere is important in our lives, it has become immeasurably powerful when compared to the right hemisphere. The right side of our brain is where beauty and art and music lie. It is also where a sense of "oneness" is perceived. Dr. Jill Bolte Taylor said it beautifully in her book, *A Stroke of Insight*.

> "To the right mind, no time exists other than the present moment, and each moment is vibrant with sensation...To our right mind, the moment of *now* is timeless and abundant...The present moment is a time when everything and everyone are connected together as *one*. As a result, our right mind perceives each of us as equal members of the human family...It perceives the big picture, how everything is related, and how we all join together to make up the whole."[6]

The right hemisphere has thus a completely different way of perceiving the world. Where the left brain prefers to view information in pieces bound by time, the right hemisphere understands that physical boundaries are only perceptions. In other words, the right brain may see reality as it really is.

The universe is infinite and we only know one little part of what lies in the cosmos. But because the left brain is so fixated on the concrete, it cannot understand the concept of infinity. The only way the left brain can somehow make sense of things is to cut it up into small pieces. If we choose to see this world solely based on the prism of the left brain, what remains is only a little of the truth. We then proceed to make that tiny piece of infinity everything there is and start labeling things that fall outside of it as wrong. Suddenly, we become self-righteous based on our little piece of infinity. We are right and the other is wrong. How can I be self-righteous when my brain is interpreting only a tiny fraction of infinity and calling that reality?

When you descend into the depths of the ocean at night, you have a flashlight to guide the way through the darkness.

The ocean is pitch black at night so you must choose where to shine your light. If I choose to shine the light ahead, I can see about ten feet in front of me. I see fish, maybe some coral, maybe one or two big fish. But what is shining under my flashlight is only a microcosm of what lies in the ocean. Can I therefore say I know what lies in the water simply because my limited beam is focusing on a few specimens of the underwater world? Of course not. In fact, while I point my flashlight ahead, I may miss the huge manta ray that is swimming right next to me or be completely unaware that there is a shark right behind.

Now suppose I finish my dive and start up a conversation with another diver on the boat, while we remove our gear. The other diver happened to flash his light on the shark. "That shark was huge!" I respond in disbelief. "What shark? Are you crazy? There was no shark out there!" Suddenly, we are arguing about two distinct truths, each one a different piece of infinity that was observed. This diving scenario can be applied to virtually any argument you have with your spouse, a friend, or a co-worker. We have altercations based on what piece of infinity we happen to have in our left brain. And don't think this is a small issue. Wars are being waged right at this moment, based on who possesses "truth," yet very few are aware of the fact that we are fighting over the tiniest fraction of information.

When you sit back in the seat of awareness and recognize that you possess only a tiny bit of the cosmos, you will notice something transformational happens. You stop thinking you are always right. Zen master Seng-ts'an said it best: "Do not seek the truth; only cease to cherish opinions." You may not realize just how powerful these words are, so read them again. When I cease to cherish opinions, I cease to look at people based on their mental models. I stop defining others based on their past pain. But more than this, I also cease to hold my own opinion in such high regard that I need to defend myself from others. I begin to understand another fundamental truth: I am no better than anyone else. Sure, you may be nodding your head in agreement, but I challenge you to think about this further.

If you get into a heated argument with someone and you think only you possess the truth and only you are right, what is the result of that type of thinking? If you are right and the other person wrong, your ego feels superior. You feel better about yourself when you make another person wrong. Does this seem like the language of the soul? Not at all. The soul is love and infinite consciousness. The soul need not be defended, for it knows the truth. Your little devil, your ego, has again sucked you into the drama it likes to create. Don't let yourself be drawn into drama. Stay in the seat of awareness and just observe the mental dramas from a distance. Instead of instinctively defending yourself you can say, "Okay, I concede I may be wrong. Do you?" When you are sitting in Awareness, the world really does start to look different. You begin to see things you never thought possible. Suddenly, you understand why your boss behaves horribly towards you. You see why the impatient driver behind you keeps honking in anger. You realize why your friend said something hurtful to you. You finally see that people do and say certain things based on their pain. You can actually see their pain. The result of this 'seeing' is that you now respond to these situations and people with different eyes—you respond with 'new eyes.' When you are able to perceive the pain in others, you begin to feel compassion and kindness. And that is magical.

Now, you may be thinking, "who cares if I see their pain? They are still treating me horribly." And perhaps you are right. Maybe your change in awareness does nothing to alter their behavior towards you or others. But that is not the point. The point here is that when you become aware, you change yourself. No transformation can occur until we transform ourselves first. Rather than worrying about whether your change in awareness will impact the behavior of others, just notice how the transformation changes you within. If you see that your friend is using her mental model during an argument with you, you stop feeling the need to defend yourself. When you do that, you will experience actual physiologic changes in your body. Your blood pressure will stay low, your heart rate normal, your levels of stress hormones remain healthy.

When you choose not to escalate the argument, you are basically giving your body a few more years of life! So does it matter whether your friend changes her behavior towards you? Have you not already made a significant impact on your own life by choosing not to get involved in your mental dramas? I think so. But there's more. I think you may be surprised to find that when you change your energy and become aware, others tend to follow or at least start to question their mental models a bit. If you choose not to argue back, you are basically deflating your friend's anger as if it were a balloon. She will literally feel your energy and it will affect her.

Noted spiritual leader Panache Desai uses the following example to illustrate how energy affects others in fundamental ways. He says that if you place two tuning forks next to each other and strike the first, the second will carry the same sound frequency. Our bodies are exactly the same. When we have brunch with a negative friend, we take on her dense energy and feel it in our body. Likewise, your decision to change your own energy will impact others. Yet the real reason you want to become aware is to live a happy, drama-free life. You get to know what inner peace really feels like. But the wonderful byproduct of becoming aware is that you inadvertently begin to change those around you. And that is really how we transform the world.

By late 2011, I was trying to transform my outer world. I had made the mistake about my career move. I didn't want to be a physical therapist anymore, but I had no idea where to go from there. So I decided to rely upon my greatest source of worth: my intellectualism. As a result, I decided to pursue a Masters of Business Administration (MBA), universally considered the benchmark degree for anyone with pretentions at entrepreneurship or corporate life. My ego told me I wanted to enter this world. But my soul is that of a healer's. What the heck was I thinking? It's a classic dichotomy. When our minds are in command, we silence the rumblings of the unhappy soul. My wife was honest with me from the start. I would explain with excitement my plans for going into business or perhaps even consulting with a healthcare consultancy firm and she would smile softly. "I just don't think an MBA is you," she would say. "But my beloved," I would insist, "I can leverage my experience in health care and move it to the next level, into business. I really think it's a great plan."

And so, I immersed myself in studying for the GMAT—the computerized test that all MBA applicants must take in order to get into a decent business school. I studied for a month and when test day arrived, walked nervously down the street to a testing center in downtown DC. I arrived early and sat next to a few other prospective MBA students in a tiny, claustrophobic waiting room with no natural light. They looked more stressed out than I did. One girl was feverishly going through her notes, hoping the words would sink in last minute. I looked over at her, trying to catch her eyes so I could telepathically send over my thoughts: "Breathe, you're going to be okay." But she was too busy to even notice my presence. It was at this moment that I sensed how much calmer I was than all those around me. I was smart and had never had the slightest problem with a test, so perhaps that was why. If there was one thing I could always rely upon, it was the power of my intellect.

Three hours later, I emerged totally humiliated. I had completely bombed the test. As I walked down the street, my head spun out the drama. "How is it possible for someone who has always excelled academically," I asked myself, "to royally screw up a computerized test?" The answer came quickly. "Because you aren't as smart as you thought are you?" I was so angry at myself, at the world in general, that I am pretty certain I would have punched someone if they had looked at me sideways. I masked my humiliation with anger. After all, my mind had just lost the 'intellectual' label. I felt completely lost because that pillar broke. My lofty self-image, built on academic attainment and the applause of others, was starting to crumble. The universe was giving me a choice— turn left or turn right—but my mind, my ego, was caught up in the illusion of control.

Here's the thing about forks in the road. They go one way or the other. There is no third 'status quo' option that lets you blindly meander along as you had been doing. The key is for us to remain aware and alert to see it, watch for the signs and listen to our souls. A big part of that moment is listening intently and letting go of the noise, confusion and bustle of the past, of our previous way of doing things, our pain and hurt and defensiveness. If we live immersed in our minds, we will continue to bang our heads against the signpost at the fork in the road, ignoring the choices before us. I know, because that is exactly what I did. I got home and promptly reregistered to take the GMAT. By the time I slipped my key into our front door, I decided that no stupid computerized test would keep me from my goal.

Two months later, I was back at the same downtown testing center, retaking the test. My little devil was insistently poking at me, saying "You'd better nail it this time or else." Or else what? As it turned out, I did even worse than the first time, somehow managing to decrease my overall score significantly. And let me tell you, that takes a pretty special effort. I can laugh about it now, but at the time, my sense of worthlessness threw me into chaos. I wore my intellectual attainments like a crown and it was being trampled in the dust. Dry mouthed and on the verge of tears, I actually waited to text my wife and tell her of the news. She was academically brilliant and professionally successful. How would I be able to tell her I had failed at something? "It's okay, my love," she responded kindly. "The GMAT is a really hard test." But her words didn't reassure me. There was really nothing she could say. My inner world had come crashing down in ways I couldn't even articulate.

Suddenly, I began to feel small around Catherine. So many of us feel this way, as if we are being eclipsed by those around us. But the truth is, you only feel small when you are empty inside. Someone who loves themselves and is secure in their worth need not compare themselves to anyone else. The fallacy of 'comparison' only happens in your mind and is another way for you to derive a sense of worth from your external environment. But why do you need to define yourself based on what's happening around you? Has it ever occurred to you that you already are good enough? Do you have any idea of the depth and love and energy that you possess? Do you know that you contain the universe within you? I know it may be hard to believe that we are all we need, but it's true. You are priceless just as you are. Go ahead, say it: "I AM priceless just as I am." I want you to hold this affirmation in your soul, in your heart and in your mind.

By the end of 2011, I was still ignoring my soul. I was angry and focused on self-deprecating thoughts. Despite my woeful test results, I still applied to MBA programs and a dual MBA/MPH (Master of Public Health) degree at Johns Hopkins University. My mind was focused on business and so the prospect of doing just a degree in public health was not appealing. I really didn't see any use for it, but I figured a dual degree would add even more initials to my name! It would be a way of rebuilding the intellectual label. Not surprisingly, the MBA programs weren't interested. But I did receive an email from the Johns Hopkins School of Public Health. "We regret to inform you that you did not get in to the MBA portion of the dual degree, but we would like you to consider the MPH. You have been accepted into the program and we hope you will attend this coming year." As I read the email, my heart sank. Rejected for the one thing that would prop up my self-image, I felt adrift. I forwarded the email to my wife and she responded with a little life raft: "Yay! You got into the MPH program. Aren't you excited? You got into the number one public health school in the world!" I was so immersed in the whole MBA debacle that I missed the part about being accepted into Johns Hopkins' world-class master's degree. It was all my mind needed to hear. And just like that, my self-worth bounced back. I was going to a top school and that meant I could hold on to the most important label I had.

It sounds insane to admit now, but I spent $80,000 on a degree my soul did not want. I pushed for something my soul knew was not right. But we all do this to some extent. We've all battled against the world to get something we think we need. Our lives should not be spent fighting for anything. Our lives are powerful and have a life of their own. Once you decide to understand your soul language and let it guide you, it becomes clear how life unfolds naturally. It happens without a tussle. When you have to fight to achieve something—and I don't mean better health care for a sick child, equal pay for women or environmental change—it can be a sure sign that you're butting up against that fork in the road. Fighting to get something means perhaps you have allowed your mind to command instead of your soul. You may disagree since popular culture prizes the scrappy fighter who risks everything for his dreams. History loves a fighter, too. Don Quixote tilted at windmills. The artist Vincent Van Gogh, who famously cut off his own ear and later ended his life, once remarked that "as we advance in life, it becomes more and more difficult, but in fighting the difficulties, the inmost strength of heart is developed." And everywhere we look, we're told "if it's worth it, it's worth fighting for."

Yet I invite you to think about this a bit more. Have you ever fought for something so hard and then when you get it...you feel empty? Why? Could it be that what you were fighting for wasn't something you needed in the first place? Wonderful, you got the million dollar home. Congratulations! Now those around you will know your monetary value—but do they know your worth? All too often, we fight for external things that will define us. We battle for things we think will somehow make us feel better about ourselves. That's why it's a fight, because it's something the mind has decided is important. You have probably heard of the guy who worked non-stop in order to live a certain lifestyle and then died of a heart attack while relaxing in his hot tub overlooking the ocean. As Oscar-winning film producer (and Oscar and Golden Globe-winning actress Helen Mirren's husband) Taylor Hackford once remarked, "You make your own choices, and what you're always fighting is ego."

19 THE SEAT OF AWARENESS

Throughout 2012, I had more lessons to learn. I had decided to go to Johns Hopkins and pursue an MPH, even though my soul had made clear it wasn't the right thing. Yet, my mind had built this infallible structure that was the foundation for my self-worth. By doing that degree, those extra letters after my name would make me happy and accomplished. Of course, the mind's models aren't all bad, far from it. The mind is an integral part of who we are, what we can dream and yes, what we can achieve. But as Mark Twain once said, "too much of anything is bad, but too much good whiskey is barely enough." I'm not going to make judgments on Twain's views on whiskey, but allow me to elaborate further on the first part of the quote.

Imagine the mind as water. It flows around obstacles, responding to outside influences and shaping them, too. The mind is not only critical to live, but it exerts enormous influence over our decisions and responses. But if the mind is not balanced with heart and soul, its power can drown us. Suppose your brain keeps you up at night for two hours a week. By year's end, you will have wasted 104 hours of your life on pointless mind chatter. By the time you are 40 years old,

4,160 hours have been spent creating mind movies in bed. If you live to reach 80, you've burned through 8,320 hours of your life. That is almost one whole year gone. Contemplate this. Do you think it is evolutionary to waste a year of your life on nothing?

Now, you may saying, "Wait a minute. Thinking isn't a waste of time!" Well, you are partly right. Thinking is not a waste of time when it leads to something concrete in your life. We think when we work. We think when we are challenged by a relationship, a puzzling scenario, a good book or an enthralling movie. That's what the mind is for. But the incessant chattering of the mind is seriously damaging. Your body is exhausted, wanting to rest. And yet your brain refuses to comply with this fundamental biological requirement. It's usually not difficult for someone to recognize that their mind causes suffering because we have all experienced this. At some point in our lives, we have all understood—even if for just a few seconds—that mind chatter does not represent who we are at our core. If so much of what we think is pointless and unnecessary, why does the mind generate all these thoughts in the first place? In *The Untethered Soul,* Michael Singer writes:

> "The secret to answering this question lies in understanding why it says what it says when it says it. For example, in some cases the mental voice talks for the same reason that a teakettle whistles. That is, there's a huge buildup of energy inside that needs to be released. If you watch objectively, you will see that when there's a buildup of nervous, fearful, or –desire-based energies inside, the voice becomes extremely active...That voice talks because you are not ok inside, and talking releases energy."[7]

For the vast majority of people, the brain's chatter never ceases. Some people who reach a deep meditative state can slow or even halt the mind's busy antics, at least for a spell. But for most of us, the mind churns through it thoughts, impressions, reactions and assessments like a hamster on a wheel. There is nothing wrong with this, because our brains are just doing what they always do. Don't attempt to stop thoughts. You'll only get more frustrated and angry at yourself. But hope is not lost. Although your mind is constantly talking, there is one skill you can acquire that will decrease the chatter significantly and thereby change your life completely. You simply stop identifying with the endless thoughts in your head or allowing yourself to be drawn into the dramas your brain creates. It's almost like being drawn into a dream and thinking you are living in reality. So how do you get out of the dream? More importantly, how do you even know you are in a dream or mind drama in the first place? Become aware. Or as I like to call it: Sit in the seat of awareness.

You sit in the seat of awareness just like you would sit in a movie theater. When you are sitting in a theater— especially in a 3D surround sound room—you can become immersed in the film. But even if you sit there for three hours staring at the screen, there is always a part of you that knows you are not really in the movie. Despite jumping at every frightening moment or tearing up when the hero dies, you never totally suspend disbelief. That is essentially what it means to be aware. Let your thoughts wash over you like scenes in a movie, just sit back with some popcorn and watch the drama unfold. Being aware means you always know you are watching a movie, even if it's in your own head.

Of course, getting to the point where you can choose to be a watcher of your mind's drama requires practice. Just when you decide that you are going to become aware, life will test your resolve. Maybe your boss publicly berates you at your desk and with every word like a blow, you feel yourself getting sucked into the stream of thoughts bombarding you. Your ego, like so much else, will go into a 'fight or flight' reflex. Sometimes, it will act like a guard dog, attacking and defending when provoked. In that moment, you feel a strong force pulling you toward the drama. Your mind is busy thinking, "what a bitch!" or "this is so unfair, I'm going to let her have it." Thoughts are very powerful and they will draw you in to them if you let it happen. But you can choose not to. You can choose to stay sitting down in your theater chair—aware that you are watching a movie about your boss.

Throughout the day, the scenes will change. In one scene, a guy cuts you off on the freeway. In another, a friend gets upset with you. Another might be someone complimenting you for kind actions. Sitting in the theater chair, you will notice that being aware gets easier and easier with each passing event. And pretty soon nothing will rock your consciousness away from that chair. Nothing will draw you in to the movie, not even the most traumatic events in your life. If your mind is successful at drawing you into its dramas, it becomes hard to leave. I am reminded of Leonardo DiCaprio in the movie *Inception*. The plot centers on dreams and how they are so real that sometimes the characters can get stuck in this make-belief world without even knowing it. So what do we do if our minds have tricked us into getting up from the theater chair and walking right into the movie screen? The most important sign is the increase in emotions.

Let's go back to your boss publicly criticizing you at work. The whole episode is playing in a loop in your brain as you're trying to drift off to sleep. With each repetition of the episode, you feel yourself getting angrier at how you were treated. Notice right away that the increase in anger is a sure sign that you are immersed in your brain's drama. If you were aware, you would have taken note of your thoughts and at that moment, would have sat back to watch the movie. Watching the movie does not increase emotion; participating in it does. So next time your brain keeps you up at night, sit back and relax. Let the brain think all it wants, but choose to be the watcher of thought, not an active participant in the dramas being created inside your skull. If you do this, you will soon fall asleep, rocked by the lullaby of mind chatter.

Back in 2012, as I immersed myself in the challenging 11-month master's degree, I started to understand the difference between 'facing obstacles' and 'fighting' for something. I distinguish between the two because I don't want to give the impression that we can sit on the couch and wait for things to fall our laps. In other words, letting life unfold does not mean being passive. Letting life roll on its path is not an excuse to become lazy. Although fighting for something may be a sign the soul doesn't want that achievement or attainment, the same cannot be said of facing obstacles. Encountering them does not necessarily mean we are doing something that is against our soul or essence. Rather, it could be a slight course correction that life sent your way. Or it may be an event that has challenged your mental model and encouraged you to grow. The fundamental difference between an obstacle and a fight is in how you feel about it. Steve Jobs encountered many obstacles while trying to build the best Apple gadgets. But he felt certain of his path and so looked upon obstacles as exciting challenges to be overcome. In other words, he felt fulfilled in his life, perhaps even because of the challenges he faced. Now compare his experience to someone who works at a job he hates, but makes him a lot of money. He dreads getting up every day and feels unfulfilled in his life. His work brings constant stress and his personal life suffers as a result. Getting out of bed in the morning feels like a fight. He may have a Ferrari and the big house by the ocean, but that does nothing to change how he feels inside. He has to use his tremendous will power to carry on, constantly fighting against life itself.

I learned what fighting against life meant when I went back to school. I have always been a student at heart. I love learning new things. Yet when I started my master's degree, I felt exhausted. I was struggling, swimming against a strong current. Every single day, I would get up and wonder, "What the heck am I doing at Hopkins?" I spent the daily train rides from DC to the Baltimore campus trying to reconcile the negative emotions I felt inside. "It's okay, you're just older and going back to school is stressful." But no matter what excuses my mind devised, I felt more and more empty as the months progressed. I was living proof that when we do not listen to the soul's language, we end up suffering. My mind had decided that school would be great for me, because it could reinforce my intellectual label. Yet I fought to get good grades. Unlike my past experiences, academic life was a real struggle. How did someone who had always excelled academically suddenly find themselves fighting for decent grades? Life whispered back, "Because you didn't listen to your soul in the first place. Everything is a struggle when you don't listen to the real you."

By autumn 2012, my household was falling apart. My wife and I seemed to be living completely separate lives. Well, perhaps we always had. We lived with so much fear in our hearts that we closed them a little bit more every time we poked at each other's wounds. And we were poking at them more and more each day. With the craziness of our lives, we didn't take the time to really get to the bottom of our pain. We had always used each other as a safe haven, often saying, "You are my home." And it was true. My wife had always been my rock and our love was the only constant in a changing world. But the problem with using others as your safe haven is that you choose to fall into their arms instead of falling into your own. Anytime you use someone—or something—to feel good about yourself, you are in for some trouble. This would all make sense to me a few months later, but by the end of 2012, I just felt like an empty tank. I had nothing left to give my spouse because I was so empty inside. I was so immersed in hating myself that I didn't even look around to see my marriage was crumbling.

The truth is that you cannot give to another that which you do not have for yourself. I wasn't giving my wife love, compassion or kindness. And the same applied to her. We were struggling in our lives and refusing to communicate our pain to each other. That's just the way we had always done things, each of us feeling alone and forced to solve our problems by ourselves. That clearly doesn't work, since marriage is a partnership, not a solo act. We should have come together and discussed our struggles. But I suspect the two of us knew that our struggles had mostly to do with our past pain, and neither of us wanted to open those wounds.

We can give only what we have. I can only give a homeless person money if I have some to give. By the same token, I can only offer love, kindness, compassion when I have them for myself. One analogy I like to use to illustrate this is the overflowing cup. Your love of self is the full cup, while your love for others is everything that overflows after the cup is filled. When you love from an overflowing cup, you love unconditionally. When you try to love from an empty cup, what you give out is a love that is conditional; it rests upon demands. You love your spouse if they do a certain thing or behave a certain way. You place conditions for loving. And when your spouse violates the conditions—and everyone does at some point, whether by omission or commission—you become disappointed and withdraw your love. The love you give others is only truly genuine when it comes from an overflowing cup. So the next time you ask, "how can I better love my spouse or friend?" you should instead start with, "how can I better love myself?"

20 LIFE GIVES AND LIFE TAKES AWAY

By the time my birthday came along in December, I was ready to explode. My cup was so empty that I was running on fumes. My wife and I had managed to talk about our general unhappiness, but we were really only dancing around the edges. We talked about issues 'between' us rather than issues 'inside' us. Our past pain and childhood traumas were so ingrained that we defaulted to focusing on more superficial things. We decided perhaps we needed some therapy in order to address our so-called communication problems. Surely all our issues would spontaneously go away if we just talked more to each other, right?

After a few sessions of therapy, it felt like we were getting nowhere. I'm not afraid of using psychotherapy. If you can find a good fit with a therapist, they can help you transform your life. Unfortunately, our marriage therapist wasn't a good fit, but we were too distracted to notice. However, he did zero in on that all-powerful issue of childhood trauma. A couple of sessions later, he hit the nail on the head. Sitting back in his chair, he looked up from his notes. "You both seem to have two people inside you," he said slowly. "A little girl who just wants to be loved and feels alone, and a big girl who thinks she can do everything by herself and doesn't need anyone."

My wife and I glanced over at each other and nodded. He was absolutely right. This insight would come in handy a couple of months later but for now, Catherine and I just weren't ready to dig deep within ourselves for the source of our problems. We continued looking for the reasons for our unhappiness in the outside environment. But at least on some level, our therapy sessions were stirring something within. On my birthday, I got a beautiful card from her that was rather prescient. The front of the card had a picture of two little girls riding together on a tricycle. The caption to the picture was a quote from Confucius that read: "Wherever you go, go with all your heart." On the inside, she wrote:

Beloved;

This year hasn't been the easiest year for either of us, with many physical, emotional, and intellectual challenges. But through it all, we've been together. And the little girl in me is riding behind the girl in you, grateful that we are on a long and wonderful adventure, one we have to share.

You are my beloved; you hold my heart. I long for each of us to break down our walls, to go deeper, in the strength of vulnerability, with trust. I trust you, Christina Marie. I know you...I love you.

With all of my heart, for all of my life,
C

When I read the card, I was struck by a thought. It was as if we weren't ready to face our individual pain. We had been mirroring each other for a long time, but we were just not prepared to look at our reflections. It was scary, painful, and dark, because looking at the mirror involved opening my heart. I had kept so much emotion and pain inside for so many years that now I felt like an old wine bottle with a corked stopper. I hadn't the slightest idea how to open my heart to her. I didn't know how to heal myself or where to even start. I was so scared of opening that door that I preferred to stand back and passively watch my marriage fall apart.

As 2013 dawned, I felt adrift, at sea with who I was and with no bearings or the slightest idea how to find my way. Catherine and I just took our mental models, past pain, childhood traumas and shoved them under the rug again. But the universe would soon put another fork in my road. On Valentine's Day, I awoke to our home filled with 14 love notes. The first one read:

Happy Valentine's Day, my Beloved. There are multiple love notes for you...find them all?
Always, Me

I spent the day looking around the house for my love notes, hidden in clever little places. I had always been afraid of life's many changes. I suppose this fear was left over from having lost two important people so suddenly and early in my life. I had become afraid of living and always expected something bad to be just around the corner. Yet, in all the fear and madness that was my life, Catherine's love represented the one constant upon which I could rely. No matter where life took us, I knew we would always be together.

Ah, life. It gives, and it takes away. Just one week after Valentine's Day, I noticed a change in Catherine. I could feel it with every cell in my body. She was physically there, but she wasn't there. I texted her on her way home from work. "Is everything okay, beloved?" She texted back. "We need to talk. I'll be home soon." When she walked in the door and up to our bedroom, where I was folding laundry, I was expecting anything except what I heard. I took one look at her closed face and instinctively sat down on our bed. My legs just lost their strength to hold my body weight up. She cleared her throat. "Tina, I don't think we should be together anymore. I haven't been happy for a long time." I was suddenly glad, very glad, that I was sitting down. My mouth went dry and I felt a wave of stress wash over me, putting me slightly off kilter, like the room had tilted imperceptibly. "That's cortisol, the fight or flight hormone," I thought, absently. I couldn't move, couldn't say anything. She hesitated, then plowed on.

"You know we've had issues for a while. I will always love you, but I just can't be married anymore." After those words, I stopped listening. I could see her mouth moving. I knew words were coming out. I just couldn't hear them. The volume was cut off. And at that moment, I felt a separation in me. I experienced what all the great spiritual teachers talk about when they refer to "being the watcher of thought." My senses were all taking in what she was saying. But there was a deeper part of me that was observing her and at the same time, observing my own mind. I felt like I was watching Catherine have a conversation with her wife and I was a third party, observing it all. I saw the whole scene without judgment.

Yet this deep peace would not last very long. "Please say something," she said, forcefully. "Be angry at me." With these words, I felt my awareness get sucked back into my mind. And the momentary peace I'd felt began to give way to profound pain. I looked up at her, then looked away. My voice sounded like it was coming from down a long hallway, disembodied from the pain I could feel building behind my eyes and in my stomach. My vocal cords contracted and I uttered the only words I could muster at this very moment. "I really want to know why my karma in this life is loss." With that, she turned and walked out of my life.

PART II: OVER THE EDGE

"This above all: to thine own self be true;
And it must follow, as the night the day,
Thou canst not then be false to any man."

Shakespeare

21 THE HEART IS CRACKED OPEN

I had spent many years with my heart closed in hopes of protecting myself and avoiding pain. Yet here I was at the age of 34, in more pain than I ever thought it possible to feel. In my panic, I couldn't think of one close friend in DC, so I called Jeets in New York. "Get on a train now," she said. "There's no reason to be in DC." And that's exactly what I did. I hailed a cab and went straight to Union Station, in downtown DC.

As the train I'd boarded clickety-clacked its way to New York City, I realized how misguided my mental model was throughout my life. Closing my heart hadn't protected me from pain. Instead, I had spent most of my life in pain because my heart was closed. I filled myself with darkness and let it overflow. I let my pain and accumulated suffering fill my heart to a point where I had become unable to love fully and with abandon. The mental model that had helped me survive as a child was now causing me to lose the love of my life, my best friend, my beloved.

I sat up abruptly. Finally, I understood. My pain and suffering had never been outside of me. It wasn't caused by my dad, my mom, my brother or my wife. I was the author of my life. At every painful juncture, when the universe gave me an opportunity to change, I stayed closed. I chose fear and panic. I wasn't alone, either. We often choose pain over wellbeing if that's what we know best, even when it causes hurt. To try something new can be temporarily more painful than sticking with old patterns.

In the days that followed the collapse of my marriage, I had many moments of clarity. I was in excruciating pain and I was broken open. This time, my suffering was so deep that it completely cracked my mental model and exposed it for the lie it created, the illusion of control. While all this chaos was brewing inside, the outside was no less problematic. Catherine and I had just bought a home together and I was entering the last three months of my master's degree. I had a thesis to write. I also felt trapped because, as a full-time student, I had no income and was financially dependent on Catherine. What on earth was I going to do? Mercifully, she made sure to put her busy travel schedule to good use. She was rarely home these days and when she was, would sleep in the guest bedroom downstairs. The whole situation was unbearable. But there was something deep within that was keeping me afloat. Every day, there was a gentle whisper in me. "You have work to do."

The cork was off the bottle. For days, my little devil had been whispering in my ear, "I told you she would leave you. Everyone leaves you." Yet this time, there was something profoundly different in me. Years earlier, I'd blamed myself for not protecting my father and being there to watch over his health. I held myself accountable. Yet in truth, his death was due to many complicated factors, none of which had to do with me. This was different. I was losing my wife. I shared half of the responsibility for our marriage's failure. Ironically, the failure of my marriage had been just as sudden as all my other losses. I started to think. "What is the universe trying to teach me? Why have I attracted situations of loss in my life?" The more I wondered, the more things became clear.

Meanwhile, my ego was valiantly trying to distract me from these profound questions with fearful thoughts. "You're alone and have no money. You're worthless and this will happen again. What are you going to do with your life? You're not going to be able to finish your degree. You don't have the strength to finish your thesis in the middle of all this mess." These thoughts just repeated themselves day and night. Every day, my ego tried to rebuild the dam by devising possible plans. "You should quit your degree and just get your old job back. At least you can start making money fast." But this time I would not allow it. This time, the fraud that my mind had created was just too obvious to ignore. I had spent the better part of my life letting my mind protect me from suffering, yet what did that get me? Suffering. As I reflected, I would see so clearly that in "protecting" me from pain, my mind had actually created immense suffering. Now, everything started to make sense.

You cannot let your mind protect you from pain. It's impossible, because there are just too many events in life for the mind to calculate. Hamlet—and by extension, Shakespeare—knew of which he spoke when he asked, "Whether 'tis nobler in the mind to suffer the slings and arrows of outrageous fortune / Or to take arms against a sea of troubles, And by opposing, end them?" The answer is no. Control over the events life throws at you is an illusion. And by the grace of God, I finally got it. When your mind protects you against pain, it knows this is an insurmountable task. As a result, you feel fear and panic. The result of maintaining the illusion of control in your life is that you live it in fear. You are literally afraid of life.

Fear. I'd known it intimately for the better part of three decades. I kept it inside me as if it were my best friend, my trusted companion. But best friends don't hurt you like this. I had *chosen* to emanate the energy of fear my whole life. I could excuse the little girl who was afraid because she didn't understand. But what about the adult? Why did the adult me choose every day to hold on to an emotion that had clearly caused so much pain? And more importantly, now that I was forced into yet another intersection in the road, would I again choose fear?

There are spectrums of energies in the universe, with fear on the denser side and love on the lightest side. Everyone has to choose between the two. Fear and love have such different frequencies, they cannot cohabitate. Fear is heavy and when you choose to emanate it, you get heavy experiences back. You literally manifest in the physical world the energy you are emanating. As I lay in bed one night, petting my beloved Great Dane, Xena, that was the message I heard from the universe. "Choose. If you want to stop losing, then stop choosing fear over love."

My eyes snapped open and I looked straight to the dark ceiling in my room. I started to cry. I sobbed, my body wracked with grief, my voice howling in convulsions, tears and snot streaming down my face. For days, I cried, more than I thought it possible. I felt as if I was crying every single tear I had held inside for three decades. I was crying for my cousin JP, my father, my mother, my brother, the little girl I was inside, my pain, my wife, and for...my life. As I reviewed my whole life, as I waded through my sorrow and slowly came up through that morass of fear and anguish, I began to feel it was "time." It was time to grow. It was time to evolve. I finally wanted to take responsibility for my life. I needed to apologize to it for having taken so long to awaken. I apologized to my body for having treated it so poorly. I apologized to my mind for giving it the impossible task of protecting me from pain. And finally, I apologized to God, to Source, for having chosen fear. I apologized to God for staying away from her for years, even though she loved me infinitely. I realized that God is pure love, nothing else. I finally saw that when you choose to emanate denser energies like fear, you choose to live separated from the source of all life. The choice is always yours: do you want to live in fear or do you want to live in love?

I suddenly understood so many things. I knew I would not be able to emanate love until I loved myself first. And I understood that the only constant in life is change. The trouble is, after so many years of listening to my devil, I drew a blank on how to love myself. How do you switch gears from self-hatred to self-love? How do you turn around a lifetime of self-doubt and self-loathing? How do you transition from "I fear" to "I love"? You do it the same way you used to get to self-hatred in the first place: one step at a time. We don't just wake up one day hating ourselves. We develop that sentiment over multiple life experiences. I remember I became aware of feeling self-hatred the day my father died, but the emotion had been there long before. With every event in my life that caused some sort of disappointment in me, my sense of self-worth dropped. And so it made sense that the road to self-love would require multiple moments of kindness toward myself. This may seem trivial, but it really is the way to love yourself. One little gesture at a time.

Of course, my second revelation that the only constant in life is change came much easier. The Greek philosopher Heraclitus (c 536 BC – 475 BC) was the first in the emerging Western world to note that "everything changes and nothing stands still." So I knew it on an unconscious level, but now, I was aware of it, like I was aware of breathing. Weeks later, while resting my soul in the wilderness of northern California,

I scribbled a few lines about my insight.

What do you do when you are standing on a rock, surrounded by streams of lava? What do you do when a step in any direction triggers your pain? What do you do when you have chosen to let your pain fill you, instead of love? Well, you can choose to stay standing, motionless. At least for a little while longer. But how torturous that is. To stay motionless in a Universe that is constantly expanding. To stay motionless while life continues—constantly changing and dancing to the rhythms of the Cosmos. What is more painful then: to stay motionless or move?

Sure, stepping off your rock and into the lava will hurt. But have you ever considered the possibility that this lava is imagined? What if the lava is instead a streaming river—leading to many joyful stops before culminating in the ocean? What if what you perceive to be lava is in fact your ticket to freedom?

So there you have it. You can continue to stand motionless on your little rock, surrounded by the unknown. Or you can step into that unknown and see where it leads. You can step toward what may hurt and arrive at freedom.

My soul wanted to be free. I wanted to be comfortable with the unknown, to accept what life sends me and to live with an open heart. But that would take some help from the 'other side.'

22 KEEPING MY HEART OPEN

As the days turned into weeks after my separation, my heart remained an enormous, open wound. But I would not close it. That decision had already been made. No matter what other pain life sent me, I was resolute on facing it with an open heart. Since living with a closed heart had caused me so much pain and not prevented loss, I was decided to do something different. I had nothing to lose. One night, I sat up in bed and proclaimed to the heavens: "I CHOOSE LOVE! Can you hear me? I CHOOSE LOVE!" Xena lifted her head, nosed my hand sleepily and drifted back to sleep. I rubbed her big, floppy grey ears and murmured an apology for waking her. Like many 'pet parents', my dog is like my child; I don't know what I would have done in those painful weeks without her.

I resumed staring up at my ceiling in the darkness. I started talking out loud to someone I had admired as a young choir girl: Jesus. I didn't really know why I found myself asking for Him since I had long been more interested in Buddhism than Christianity. Yet, I noticed I wasn't talking to the Jesus in the Bible, I was asking to know someone altogether different. I wanted to talk to the being who walked the earth, the man who represented the evolution of consciousness, the man who showed us all that evolution and Source is within, not without.

Before long I realized something else. I couldn't live with half an open heart. In choosing love over fear, I would have to address the one thing that fear had kept riveted shut, ever since I was a little girl 'seeing' and feeling what others did not. I would now willingly throw open the portal to other realms. I decided to be true to myself. I stared at the ceiling for a few more seconds and then closed my eyes. My body began to feel light, peaceful. I noticed my breathing slowed down. Yet, I wasn't asleep or even sleepy. I was feeling such deep peace but at the same time, was as alert as can be. I let this foreign sensation in my body progress. There was a trust in me now and no fear. After a few minutes of silence and still with my eyes closed, I started talking out loud to Jesus. "I don't know how to come up to you, so please come get me and show me what you want." That very moment, I felt his energy. It was as if I knew this person. I kept my eyes shut. Suddenly, I felt his energy pull me up in the air. My physical body was still lying on my bed in the dark, face up and hands relaxed at my side. But although my body looked like I was napping, my consciousness was flying.

That first night, I simply felt my consciousness detach from my physical body and drift over my bed. I knew my body was resting peacefully on the bed, but my awareness was elsewhere. It was actually floating around the room, as if I was seeing life from a completely different perspective. Remarkably, I wasn't scared at all at the separation from my physical body. It felt sort of like taking your robe off and hanging it while you shower. You know the robe is there, just waiting for you to finish your shower before reaching for it again. I knew that my connection with my body was there and available. How I knew this is hard to explain. It's as if I acquired more knowledge outside of my physical boundaries. I just knew more when I was free of my brain.

Each subsequent night, I would go through the same routine. I'd lay on my bed with little or no light, rest my hands peacefully by my side, close my eyes and ask for Jesus. And each night, I would go further, flying higher and higher. As my out of body wanderings increased in altitude, so, too, did my visualizations of Jesus. One night, I flew with Him over the clouds. He was holding my hand and I could see it clearly. But his face was not visible—it looked like a photo-shopped picture. With each sequential event, I went higher. Oddly, there were always two states that I felt deep within: love and peace. I wasn't scared one little bit. It felt so weird that I was going through this remarkable experience, yet the one emotion that had always accompanied me throughout life was missing. I wasn't complaining about the lack of fear. It was just so obviously ironic that I didn't feel it now, while floating around the skies! There were only two people who knew what was happening to me: my soul sister Sandra and my mother's older sister, aunt Eva.

While all this craziness was happening to me at night, I still had to keep it together during the day. Life didn't stop because Catherine had left me. I still had groceries to buy, a dog to walk, a degree to finish. But something wasn't right. I became so physically ill that I had to stay home some days, unable to shake the nausea and general malaise. I lost weight quickly, suffered from vomiting and diarrhea and had no idea how to stop it. How could I feel so strong and full of purpose emotionally and spiritually, while my body deteriorated?

I had good days and not-so-good days. On my bad days, I would just try to gather my strength and be centered—no more flying. But after a while, I regained some strength and decided to call on Jesus once again. This time, I flew higher than I ever had before. We went into the upper atmosphere, past the thin line that separates space from our atmosphere and beyond. We arrived at two doors. The one on the left was dull colored, like it had lived in the rain for too long. The one on the right was golden. Without a word being spoken, I understood that I had to choose. Initially, I opened the one on the left and immediately saw darkness and felt a dense heaviness come over my body. Terrified, I closed the door quickly. I looked to my right and saw the golden door again. This time I brought my face very close. It had a beautiful and intricate design on it—I reached out to pass my fingers over the surface details. It felt wonderful, so I opened the door.

What was on the other side was glorious. Before me was an endless field of tall grass, with a perfectly blue sky above. One tree stood in the middle. This world—or vision—contained a sun, disproportionately large enough to kiss the ground. I could have reached out and touched it, too. Without hesitating, I walked around the field and ran my hand along the top of the grass. I felt a peace I had never felt before. I looked up and this time, I saw Jesus…I could actually see Him now. He was very tall, dressed in a white robe with a purple shawl–a tallit perhaps–around His neck. On His feet, He wore brown leather sandals. Now that my eyes were open, I could also see His face. His warm, loving smile, framed by shoulder-length, curly brown hair, extended to His eyes.

It was a strange, exhilarating and, for a scientific mind, admittedly confusing time. Was this a nervous breakdown I was experiencing? Hallucinations? Brain tumor? I considered all those rational explanations as only a scientific mind could. As I grappled for a reason, on a deeper level, I knew what I was experiencing was real. One thing I did know was that I was on a new spiritual and emotional journey—but I hadn't reached the destination yet. In many ways, I was still viewing the world largely through the lens of my ego, so my suffering was profound. I wasn't just suffering because my marriage ended. My little devil was still whispering some things I actually believed.

Meantime, my 'real' life continued to unfold. Every time I

spoke to Catherine, it felt as if there was someone else inhabiting her body, as though I was speaking to a stranger. She wanted to just part ways, quickly and cleanly. But I needed more. "I'm not prepared to call it quits this quickly and would like to do couples' therapy," I said to her, one day. She acquiesced, but during therapy, made it clear that it was to give me closure, not to work on a possible reconciliation. It was agonizing to hear some of the words she spoke and how she described our marriage. At times, it was almost too much to bear, especially when she muttered, "I hated how I felt when I was with you."

After a couple of weeks, I called my psychic Karen. She was quick to address my current life situation and particularly my health and weight loss. My body was experiencing a rapid shift in energy and that any shift upward would manifest itself in the symptoms I was experiencing. "Don't worry," she said. "Soon you will start to feel sick, your body may feel tired and your eating habits will change. Don't be afraid, it's just a change in energy. You are ascending in energy frequency and that change rocks your body a bit. But you are to maintain a high frequency of energy—it is part of your path now. Do you understand? You are to maintain a high energy. You are NOT to dip down. Do you understand me, sweetheart?" I was a little confused and asked what 'dip down' meant. "You are not to vibrate in density anymore, you are not to dip down below the energy you are meant to vibrate at." I got it. Karen had nothing to worry about. I had made the conscious decision not to vibrate in fear any longer. The density of fear would no longer weigh me down.

With each passing day, my body felt better and better. In fact, I felt great! For the first time in years, I felt like running! Now, this was definitely something new. Normally, I only run to catch a bus or while playing sports. Running just for the sake of it seemed boring and pointless. Yet I felt like I was living in a different body—a body that really wanted to fly along the earth, legs flashing in the sun and eating up the miles. Spiritually and emotionally, I felt wonderful. I felt light, as if I finally set down a heavy burden. In truth, I had been crying away my past pain and once the flood ended, I felt relieved and uplifted. I was still deeply in pain with the end of my marriage, but the pain felt different than before. Because I was choosing to keep my heart open through it all and embrace vulnerability, the pain felt lighter. My body was living proof that when you open your heart, pain becomes less intense and passes more quickly. I was learning to let all my emotions pass through me. Emotions really are 'energy in motion.'

23 COMMUNICATION WITH HEAVEN

Frustrating and hurtful as it was to go to couples therapy—I wanted reconciliation, my wife had already moved on and was seeing someone else—our therapist saw that there were deeper issues at play within each of us and promptly recommended individual therapists so we could work on our childhood trauma. And that is how I found myself sitting in a chair in Jeffrey's office. "How can I help you?" asked Jeff, as I made myself comfortable. "Well, my wife left me and our couples therapist thinks it's a good idea for us to each do some individual work before coming back to see her. So here I am." Jeff's face was impassive and he didn't talk much at first, aside from asking pointed and uncomfortable questions, then waiting in silence for me to respond. As I spoke, he started looking me up and down—as if trying to spot emotion coming out of me. I was guarded that day and, after a two hour filmed session, felt exhausted. I had been trying to open my heart as best I could, but I was taking baby steps and each one of them was difficult.

During our session, I felt the old fear creep back into me. I started wondering why on earth my couples therapist, Mary*, had recommended him. He seemed rude and a bit too blunt for me. "How does this guy manage to keep any clients?" I wondered. When we began talking about my childhood, I started to feel stirrings inside my stomach that I hadn't felt since I was a child in Portugal. "You are angry," Jeff noted. "No. I feel pain, not anger." I was also feeling a little annoyed. But he was relentless. "Really? Your wife leaves you and is sleeping with someone else and you feel 'pain'? That's it? Your mom lets her child take on the responsibility of caring for her husband and you feel 'pain'?" I felt my blood boil at his presumption spat out, "I'm feeling angry at you!" He nodded. "Good! You are feeling anger toward me! That's a start!"

Hearing Jeff talking about Mama and Catherine stirred my protective instincts. I had always sheltered those I loved, even if they hurt me. I would justify the pain by remembering that their behavior was because of their past pain, their suffering. I didn't realize that in excusing them, I was blocking my own anger from passing through me. A healthier way of dealing with it would have been to simply acknowledge that certain actions by certain people had hurt me and I felt angry about it. Just like that. No excuses necessary, no forgiveness necessary. All I had to do was acknowledge how I felt and let those emotions pass through me. Jeff taught me that on my first therapy session. And that is why I came to call him my "angel therapist."

By the time I got home, I was completely drained, but was also finally allowing the anger stored inside me to see the light of day. I paced back and forth in the house, drawing up the emotion slowly from the depths of my being. Since I believe in the therapeutic effects of writing, I quickly took out my journal and made a Top 10 list of reasons I was angry. It felt good to write these things down. Yet, when I was done, I felt the fear creep in again. Now that I was acknowledging why I was angry, I faced a new challenge: What would I now do with these powerful emotions that were coming to the surface?

I opened up our next session by asking Jeff that very question. I was trying to learn how to live with an open heart and just let emotions 'pass through', but these concepts are so much easier to read about in book than to live. Perhaps I was meant to answer this question for myself because we somehow transitioned to another topic that took up the rest of our session: my sense of worthlessness. I had been busy trying to figure out my inner world and when the time came to look at one of the darker aspects of this world, I again didn't know exactly where to start. I decided to write about it.

Drowning in Worthlessness

Have you ever witnessed someone drowning? When this unfortunate event occurs, the person becomes panicked and afraid. They try to tread water but end up swallowing more. They desperately look to land while the current pulls them away. And did you know that if you—as a bystander—jump in the water to help, you will most likely drown with the poor idiot you were trying to save? Why? Because in the panic, consumed by fear, the drowning person will claw at you so hard that both end up at the bottom of the ocean.

Now try to use the image of a drowning person and apply it to your sense of worthlessness. You see, worthlessness and drowning work in much the same way. You spend your whole life believing yourself unworthy, not good enough. Drowning in an ocean of self-hate and self-doubt. And so you desperately try to fill this internal void by looking outside of yourself. You claw at any bystander that shows up in your vicinity. Of course, you are probably unconscious to the fact that this person will end up drowning with you, unaware of how deep and dark your sense of self-hate is. Yet, you carry on with your life, drowning a little bit more every day. Taking bystanders with you. Many of these so-called bystanders are people you say you love. They are family, spouses, boyfriends, girlfriends, friends, co-workers. But my question to you is this: can you really say you love them when you are drowning them? I propose that you have no idea what love really means. Am I being too harsh?

Let's go back to the image of the drowning person. Do you think that person, consumed by fear and panic, has the capacity to feel love while desperately trying to stay above water? Do you think a drowning person can look around and contemplate the magnificence of the ocean they are drowning in? Do you think they can appreciate the beauty of the innocent bystander who jumps in the water to help them? Do you think they can see ANY beauty at all in the very moment they are drowning? The answer to all these questions is no. The only thing a drowning person can see is death, panic, darkness. And this is exactly how you live your life while drowning in worthlessness. You cannot possibly have the capacity to feel love. You miss the beauty in people and things. You miss the sweet fragrance of a rose. You miss what a sunset over the ocean looks like. In essence, you miss life.

So what can be done about this predicament? "How can I save myself from drowning in worthlessness?" you ask. It is quite simple. Become aware.

For the drowning person, awareness is that moment when consciousness bypasses a panicked brain and reminds them that swimming against the current is a stupid idea. Awareness tells them to stop fighting and let the current take them out. If the drowning person becomes aware, they will soon find that they are no longer drowning. They have simply floated away from the rip tide and are now surrounded by the calmness of the ocean. In this peace and calm, completely out of the current's grip, the person suddenly realizes they can swim safely to shore. The scary ordeal is over.

For the person drowning in worthlessness, awareness means looking inside oneself and shining light on the soul. Awareness is understanding the meaning of a bumper sticker that proclaims: "Don't always believe what you think." You are the watcher of thought. You are the consciousness that is aware of the endless voices in your head—voices that whisper, "You're not good enough. You're worthless." To be aware is to see. See what self-hate is. Look at it long and hard. Shine the light of awareness on the darkness of worthlessness. As St Paul said, "Everything exposed by the light becomes visible and everything that is illuminated becomes a light."

That is it. Once you become aware of your drowning, the ocean disappears and you will find yourself standing on solid ground. No more fear, no more panic. And now you will start to see the beauty around you. You will understand the miracles that happen every day—from the fat bumble bee that manages to fly, to the salmon that stubbornly swim upstream in order to spawn.

You are no longer drowning. You can begin to see beauty in people. There is no need to claw at them, no need to drown them with you. All that is left is space. And in this space you will feel love for the first time. Love of self and love of others.

It seems I had answered my own question. The way to process emotions was simply to shine light on them. The way to let emotions pass through you is to simply acknowledge them and open your heart. Breathe deeply, relax your body and witness emotions pass. I had stumbled upon the most important aspect of emotional release. Emotions will not process until you are ready to acknowledge their presence. But once you do, those emotions dissipate very quickly. I know you are probably thinking I'm making this all sound too easy. Well, it is and isn't. It is easy to let emotions pass through you once you have observed them clearly. Oddly, the harder part is acknowledging their presence in the first place. When we suppress emotions for any extended period of time, we stop being able to recognize them. It's similar to making a milk shake I suppose. Initially, when you put the ingredients in the blender one by one, you can easily identify them: milk, strawberries, chocolate, maybe some banana. But once you close that lid and hit the "blend" button, you become completely incapable of distinguishing one ingredient from another. That's why I had initially called my anger 'pain' when I first spoke to Jeff. I wasn't intentionally misleading him, I had just lost the ability to recognize what anger felt like because I had run it through my internal blender for many years.

Outside of my breakthroughs in therapy, I was also having some spiritual ones, too. Every day I was closing my eyes and traveling. One day, Jesus finally spoke to me. I asked Him why I was going through this pain. "So that you have faith in me. I need you to have faith in me," he explained. "Please send me a sign," I responded. "Please." Yes, call me faithless but at this point, I really did go through periods where my ego said I was losing it. "There are plenty of people talking to Jesus these days and they're mostly in psych wards." I knew those on the other side had the power to provide "manifestations" (ie, a scent left in a room, a message delivered via a friend) to those of us on this side. I knew Jesus could do the same. He could help reassure me that I wasn't indeed going crazy. So I asked for a sign.

As my travels became clearer and clearer, I started transcribing them to keep in my records. I was also allowing myself to feel whatever it was my body wanted to feel. I was finally learning how to love myself. I was being kind to myself and with each act of kindness, I felt my heart fill more and more with love. At the same time, I slowly began to feel fear creep in. Every time I closed my eyes and talked to Jesus, I kept thinking I might be crazy. The little devil on my shoulder said I was probably hallucinating. I would learn later just how fascinating the ego really is. Its foundation is control and every time it loses control, it fights for it back. This means that when there is an expansion of consciousness, when there is an evolution in your energy, the mind fights. And the main weapon used by the mind in this fight is fear. Every single time my ego said, "You're going batshit crazy," I felt fear. And in that fear there were always follow-up thoughts. "I can fix this." You see how clever that is? The ego creates fear, then it offers up a solution. And if you let your awareness be drawn into this circle, then the ego remains in control.

I wrote down everything I could remember. I didn't really know where I was going, but I assumed my field was Heaven because I felt a peace and contentment that I had never felt in life. I also felt a deep love that was absolutely unconditional. As the days progressed, I continued to have visions or travels.

04/17/13

I ascended to my field and saw that I was a child again. Jesus was running—carrying me on his back. I look to be about five or six years old. I felt a deep love for Him, as a father. In fact, today was the first time I called Him "Father." He gently pulled me down from his shoulders and hugged me. I held on so tightly to his neck that I could smell his hair.
Father: You have to go now.
I felt a deep fear come over my little body.
Me: Where am I going, Father?
Father: You have many people waiting for you.
He placed me on the ground and pointed to the horizon. I started seeing people emerge from the distance. The first person I recognized was Dad. Then I saw Vó! After that I saw my grandfather. They were all coming for me. Daddy grabbed my left hand and Vó my right. We walked away together, but before we disappeared in the distance, I turned around to see Father. He smiled at me and waved goodbye. Suddenly, I was surrounded by so many people. I could recognize my family members, but there were others I could not remember. Then, in the middle of the crowd I see a little Catherine come for me. She too looked about five or six. She smiled at me. "Let's go play! They don't need us anymore."
BOOM

When I opened my eyes, I could still feel that love very strongly, but I was disoriented. Catherine's soul had started showing up in my visions. Was I just forcing the visualizations? Was my brain playing more tricks on me? Karen had already explained to me that the soul could travel anywhere and communicate in any reality. But was I really talking to my ex-wife's soul? I remained skeptical. I had also fallen into the habit of ending my transcriptions with the word "BOOM", but had no idea why. I guess the word just conveyed to me the power of my visions. BOOM...like a bomb!

The more I thought about her appearance in my vision, the more I realized it was a releasing of old karma. The little girls in us had done their jobs. They had lived through their experiences. Now it was time to let them go. When she said, "They don't need us anymore," I believe she was referring to the adult women we had become. Indeed, we had held on to these little girls and their mental models for so many years. The little girls did what they could to survive their painful childhoods, but the mental models they had created were no longer appropriate for the adults in us. In fact, our lives had exploded precisely because we were still viewing the world and responding to it through the hurt of little girls. It was time to let them go with love and compassion. And that is what I did on that day.

I never told Jeff about my visions. How could I say, "Oh hey, what's up! I can communicate with Heaven!" As much as I loved my spiritual life, it was too new and nascent to expose to judgment, even by my therapist. So I carried on living two separate lives, which would often collide. My body was still feeling side effects of the energy shift and as a result, I had become extremely sensitive to the energy of others. At times, I would have to leave the room if they vibrated at a dense level. It was exhausting and caused me a bit of panic. Some days, I'd just lie on my couch and wonder, "Is this how I have to live the rest of my life? Will I have to run from people because they make me sick?" My longtime friend and confidante, Sandra, (or Twin, as I called her) reassured me. "Don't be afraid. You just have to learn how to protect yourself better. You have to learn how to cleanse your chakras." I half laughed at the thought. "Cleanse my chakras? What the heck are 'chakras' and why do they need cleansing?"

I knew a little about chakras or the body's "energy centers," but not nearly enough to guide me through this new phase of my life. In the Hindu tradition, there are seven chakras or vital force centers: the crown, third eye, throat, heart, solar plexus, sacral and base chakras. When chakras are in alignment, there is an equilibrium of energy coming in and out of the energy centers. The chakras are in essence, communication centers. They transmit energy outward, but also capture and process energy from the outside. When they are out of alignment, we can suffer all sorts of issues, such as physical disease, emotional, and mental problems. I came across a passage that caught my attention. "Panic attacks can sometimes be caused by a blocked heart chakra." Well then.

I was slowly starting to ask my soul what it wanted to do next. Since my life had imploded and I had decided not to let my mind rebuild the dam, I felt adrift. All my certainties had vanished. I had started listening to my soul. A faint stirring, a distant voice seemed to give me the desire to write a book. I pressed my soul for a more detailed answer. Silence. Well, maybe Heaven could help.

24 UNDER CONSTRUCTION

Although I was finishing up my degree and studying for finals, my home life was a shambles. I was hurting, but could also clearly see a difference in the intensity and duration of the pain. When you live with a closed heart, you experience pain over a longer period, at a higher intensity. With an open heart, you still experience pain because you are human and have an ego, but it is shorter in duration and reaches only medium intensity. In other words, it pays to live with an open heart because you only experience pain in short bursts throughout your life versus suffering constantly. And you can choose which way you go. I didn't change in the drop of a hat. In fact, every day presented new challenges. I was slowly learning how to let emotions pass through me, let go of my ex-wife, accept the present moment and surrender to life. I still felt fear. But mercifully, it too was coming in fast spurts that would vanish quickly. For the first time, I knew what it felt like to live free of constant fear.

04/27/13
Father: You must learn to love Catherine in freedom. You must lose that fear.
Me: But you never tell me anything. I feel a little lost.

Father: I tell you what you need to know for now. If I showed you too much of the future, you would never lose that fear. You would not want to change.

He then shifted the conversation a bit.

Father: Look at her right now. Why don't you look at her down there in the same way you see her up here? You KNOW who she is. You KNOW who she is on a very deep level. So why do you choose to see her in any other way?

I didn't have an answer for that.

Father: You know, you are choosing to look at her ego, but you are looking at it with YOUR ego. Both your egos are BIG. We need to work on that. If your ego were smaller, you would be able to truly SEE her. Her ego would not hurt you. Look at her for who she REALLY is.

BOOM

As I emerged from my travel, I thought about what Jesus said. "You must love her in freedom." I knew what he meant. To love in freedom is really to love unconditionally. A feeling that places demands or conditions is really not love at all. I admit that learning to love Catherine in this new way wasn't easy. My fears and past traumas had always influenced the way I loved people. I held on to them with an iron grip because I was scared they would either die or leave me. But "needing" someone is not love, it's attachment. The soul does not need, it simply loves. So who is it that "needs" someone or something in order to be happy? The ego. Jesus's words helped me understand an essay by Anthony de Mello. In his magnificent book, *The Way to Love*, de Mello noted this much:

> "Has it ever occurred to you that you can only love when you are alone? What does it mean to love? It means to see a person, thing, or situation as it really is and not as you imagine it to be, and to give it the response it deserves. You cannot love what you do not even see."[8]

I was choosing to see my ex-wife through the prism of my ego. It was preventing me from seeing the soul I knew so well.

04/30/13

I ascended. Father was waiting for me. We went walking in the field for a little while in silence. He wasn't talking, but was smiling.

Me: You're not going to say anything today? You're doing that on purpose, aren't you?

Father: Perhaps.

Me: You don't show me anything on purpose.

Father: Well, those who have "certainties" don't lose their fear.

Me: I don't have any "certainties" left in me Father. But you could send me proof. Couldn't you?

Father: Well, tell me what sounds like a stronger faith: when you believe after you see the proof or when you believe before it arrives? I am very pleased with you, my child, because you are feeling more and more comfortable with the idea of change. You wrote a paper for school about this idea of "impermanence." You said that the only certainty in life is change. You said people should live completely comfortable with constant change. So why don't you live what you write my child?

I started to cry.

Me: I'm still afraid.

Father: I know. But you already trust Heaven a great deal!

Me: Will you take away this fear?

Father: I'm not Superman!

He laughed out loud when he said that!

Father: You must choose, my child. Losing fear is a choice.

Me: Ok. But can you help me?

He then placed his hand on my head and I felt light enter my body.

BOOM

I was learning more and more about this 'being' that was Jesus Christ, Superstar. His energy felt almost overwhelming at times. He was funny and blunt when he needed to be. We communicated sometimes without words, simply through feelings. At other moments, I just knew He was happy about something even without looking at Him. The world of energy that surrounds us all is rather interesting. We can and do communicate with each other in so many ways that don't involve verbal interactions. Sometimes, you can just sense someone is upset at you before you see them. I was slowly learning about the consciousness that was Jesus.

Over time, I began to develop my skill of communication with the other side. My eyes trembled and shook now whenever I ascended to my field. I didn't understand what was happening to me, but the old fear was dissipating. I didn't need an explanation for my eye convulsions and in fact, as the weeks progressed, I used them as a sign that my antenna was connected. At this point, I was slowly starting to "hear" the other side in my day to day life. I was finally learning to feel comfortable with the many weird sensations I had felt since childhood. One day, while having a conversation with Twin, I heard the words, "close your eyes and redirect your gaze inward." Someone from the other side was telling Twin to look inside herself before casting judgment on anyone else. I didn't know who was speaking to me and I wasn't actually hearing words, it felt more like I was receiving blocks of thought that my brain translated. I started to refer to this phenomenon as feeling words. Instead of hearing someone say something to me, I was feeling thoughts come into my brain and turning them into words.

As I continued to develop my skill, I started to learn some key lessons. I could only talk to Jesus at a time of His choosing. I could only connect with Heaven when my ego was quiet. On days my mind was a bit more active, the connection would not occur or I would see things in a very blurry way. This was a great lesson because it proved that I wasn't just making all this stuff up in my head. If I were, then I could talk to Jesus Christ Superstar (JCS) whenever I felt like it. Furthermore, if this was all a product of my imagination, I would have no problems "connecting." On some days, I felt I was stuck in a remote location without cell phone reception. Yet throughout it all, I was learning to be kind to myself. I didn't push. I tried as best as I could to quiet my mind and close my eyes. If Heaven wanted to connect, so be it. If not, I felt okay with that. Every time I would ascend to Heaven, it seemed to change my energy. I recall looking up to the blue sky of my field and watching a portal open. JCS was there and waved to me, asking, "Do you want to come up here?" Naturally I did. I stood in front of Him surrounded by brilliant lights. I came to call this place Light Heaven, since it was located directly above my field. From there, I couldn't see anything at all except for a light so dazzling and intense, I would emerge from my travels with a headache for the first few days.

05/10/13

I ascended to an empty field. Everything was quiet. I sensed JCS was calling me to go up further so I entered Light Heaven.

Father: You're sad. You feel lonely.

Me: Yes.

Father: Then cry my child. Cry.

I fell to my knees and started to cry. Father helped me up.

Father: This solitude is necessary so you can focus on yourself. Right now, your heart is tender and sensitive and that is wonderful. But a fresh wound needs to be cared for so dirt doesn't get in it. So don't feel sad with this solitude—accept it as part of your path. It doesn't mean you must always live alone in order to have a tender heart. Not at all. It's just for now…until you practice more. With practice you will learn to live with a tender and open heart but at the same time know how to protect it from the egos you will encounter in the world.

Me: Why don't you tell me more? You want me to trust you, but you don't trust me.

Father: That's not true at all. I do trust you. You are my jewel. I need you to focus intently on the present moment. You must learn how to see things up here but also live moment by moment down there.

Me: Why is everything so…sterile up here?

Father: It's not sterile. It's light. It's love. We don't need anything else.

BOOM

25 "YOU ARE NOT A VICTIM"

Solitude. I was experiencing a lot of it since my separation. It was a self-imposed, to some extent. I was in the last days of my master's degree, preparing my thesis, studying for finals, meditating. And I was living in the same house as Catherine during it all. Life on the outside was confusing and chaotic. Keeping to myself was a way of maintaining my balance. I knew I had to keep it together until I finished school. Then after that, I was giving myself permission to melt down.

I continued to see my therapist Jeff, but had stopped with the marriage counseling. It was pointless. Catherine was determined to end the marriage and I gave up trying to convince her otherwise. We agreed that I would stay in our home until my degree was finished. Then, I would leave the house and start over somewhere else. I had no idea what to do or where to go, but my mind was simply focused on living life one day at a time. There was no room for thinking about the future when I had a thesis to finish.

"Are you coming to graduation?" a friend asked on our daily train ride to campus. "No. I don't think I could handle being there alone." I looked out the window as I said those words. Tears welled up in my eyes. I was graduating in two weeks and the person who had been instrumental through it all, my rock, would not be there. "You have us. We'll be there. Think about it." Yes, my school friends were all going to the ceremony. With their families. I envisioned what it would feel like to walk down the aisle in my cap and gown. I felt a painful knot in my stomach at the thought. Tears started streaming down my face. How deeply lonely I felt in that moment. My family lived in Portugal and California and would not be attending. Truthfully, I had downplayed the importance of this milestone in an effort to prevent anyone from coming. I didn't want to welcome family or friends in DC at that moment. I would have to answer questions, deal with their anger towards my ex-wife. I had no strength left in me for that.

The next day, I awoke with a deep sense of peace. It was as if someone had charged my emotional batteries during the night. I felt rejuvenated. Empowered. "You are not a victim." With that thought, I jumped out of bed and took a shower. My cell phone rang as I was getting dressed. It was my beloved aunt Eva, from California. "I had a vision. I am supposed to tell you to come to California. You're supposed to be with me for a while." Okay, then! When I got off the phone, something clicked. *You are not a victim.* I closed my eyes, took a deep breath and went downstairs. Catherine was working on the computer. "I'm leaving the house earlier than expected and need you to take care of Xena for a while." She seemed caught off guard. We had agreed that I stay in the house until at least after graduation, when my life was more settled and I could find a job. And we also agreed that I take full custody of Xena. But something had changed overnight. I needed to regain my footing. "Where will you go?" Catherine asked as I poured myself a cup of coffee. "That's not important," I answered, walking away. "I'll figure it out."

Three days later, my front door was filled with boxes. I was moving all my possessions into storage. A friend from school had offered me her couch a month before, but I was reluctant. Yet with my recent "click", I decided to take her up on her offer. I also decided to go to my graduation ceremony. *You are not a victim.* There was no way I was going to miss the last day of the most difficult academic year of my life. I was graduating from the Johns Hopkins Bloomberg School of Public Health. And I was damn proud of myself.

Jeets decided to come down to DC for the ceremony, so I would have someone important standing by my side. Just as I finished piling boxes at the front door, Catherine walked in. "When are you leaving?" she asked. I looked her squarely in the eyes. "Tomorrow. I'd rather you not be here when I leave. Thank you for taking care of Xena for a while." I returned to my box piling activities. She hadn't moved. "I'd like to come to your graduation if that's okay with you," she said, quietly. I was completely caught off guard and slowly put down the box I was holding. I looked at the face of the woman I once thought would be mine forever. "I don't want you there. It would be too painful." With that, I turned around and went upstairs.

The next day I moved out. I spent the morning shuttling my things to a storage unit close by. With the last box loaded into a rented van, I walked around the house in silence. I sat on the large office mat that had been my meditation spot for the last months. The office was an open space mezzanine that overlooked our living room. I looked around for a little while, then started to cry. I pressed my face to the floor and whispered, "Thank you to this house for all that it has given me." After a few minutes, I got up and walked out the front door. I closed it behind me very slowly and paused right before locking it. It wasn't just a door I was closing. An entire chapter of my life was ending and the pain increased with each turn of the key. My phone vibrated in my pocket. Catherine sent a text. "I'd like to say goodbye to you." My vision blurred and I had trouble texting back. "Today is one of the most difficult days of my life. I can't. I'm sorry." I stared at the message for a few seconds and hit send.

A week later I stood in my cap and gown, surrounded by hundreds of happy, excited classmates and their families, snapping photos, laughing and smiling. My school friends came over for a hug. "We're so glad you're here!" I couldn't say the same for myself. I took a deep breath and thought, "It's okay to feel whatever you feel. Let it be." Suddenly, my name was called out on stage. I walked up a few steps and across the stage to where the Chair of the school stood. He hugged me and handed me a tube, which contained a whole year of monumental effort. I smiled for the camera, said thank you and walked off the stage. "Tina! Tina!" My favorite professor was calling me from the mezzanine. She had been my thesis advisor and knew what had happened in my personal life. She smiled and mouthed the words, "I'm very proud of you." Tears streamed down my face as I walked out of the hall, diploma in hand. I gently took off my cap and gown, handed them over to the waiting maître d, and boarded a train straight to the Baltimore airport. As the plane took off, I was still holding that tube in my hand. With my face pressed up against the window, I cried and whispered to Baltimore, to my home in DC. "Thank you for all that you have given me." Then I fell into a deep sleep as the plane headed to San Francisco. I was so tired. It was time to rest.

26 RESTING AMONG THE REDWOODS

05/24/13

I ascended and sat down on my field in a traditional meditation position, with my legs crossed and hands gently resting on the legs. Suddenly, I was floating in the air! Father showed up in the same position and also floating!

Father: Hello, my child!

Me: Father! I haven't seen you in a while! Why?

Father: Your ego. It's still strong. I need you to spend more time meditating. I need you to focus. You are doing very well, my princess. Continue to immerse yourself in nature.

Me: And the book?

Father: The book will come when your ego is weaker. I need you a bit lighter like you are up here!

Me: But I can't float down there!

Father: But you can be light. Calm your mind.

He floated away, but stopped in the distance to say one last thing. "I need you to meditate longer. I want you light like you are here."

BOOM

I had been spending my days in the wilderness of northern California. It was so therapeutic to be amongst the great redwoods. Those trees humbled me. They were breathtakingly enormous and had been standing for decades, even hundreds of years. I felt like a little girl back on the islands. Nature really does have a way of teaching us the meaning of 'present moment' living.

The animal kingdom knows no other way except living in the now. A bird doesn't ruminate about what his mother did when he was little; the butterfly isn't thinking about where to find nectar tomorrow. Mother Nature only lives at this exact moment and no other.

Every day, I got up and went to the wilderness for a run. I now enjoyed running and couldn't wait to put on my minimalist shoes before heading out the door. Running was freeing to me. I was becoming lighter and lighter with each passing day. I knew what Jesus meant when He said He wanted me 'light.' He wasn't talking about my weight but rather, my energy. I felt every day that I was emanating a higher and higher frequency. My ego was still active. I had been trying to learn meditation because I knew it would be the best way to calm the mind. But it wasn't coming easily.

Meditation has been used for thousands of years and even now, spiritual teachers recommend it around the globe. Yet sitting still for a long period was a bit unsettling and I found myself fidgeting incessantly. I also found the meditation position was painful for my back, which focused my attention there, instead of on my breathing. However, I continued to practice kindness towards myself and refused to get upset at these little hiccups. I had started with baby steps, meditating for five minutes every day. But JCS wanted more, so I downloaded a few 20 minute guided meditations to try. If Jesus said meditation was important, I would just practice harder.

05/26/13
I ascended to the field but there was nobody there waiting for me. I started running around and my heart started shining a bright light, like a

flashlight! I felt a deep love. Just love. I started feeling my ego enter. My mind really wanted to see Father and it forced a visualization of Him. He appeared, but didn't look real. I knew it was my mind interfering. I gently asked my ego to quiet down and not force it. In an instant, Father's image disappeared and I was left alone in the field again. Suddenly, I felt my Dad! I couldn't see him yet but I could FEEL his presence so I started to cry. I turned around and saw Dad walking in my direction! He looked so handsome in his farmer's clothes. The first thing I did when he reached me was to grab his hands. I could feel his rough skin as if I were a teenager again. He stroked my face with one of his rough hands and it tickled!
Me: I miss you, Dad.
Dad: I love you so much. You have a strength that you don't even know. Live your life with an open heart, just as it is now. I'm so sorry for what I made you live through. It was my path, but I didn't mean to hurt you. Forgive me. I lived with a closed heart. I loved your mother so much and you and your brother. But I went through life without knowing how to express that. But your path is not mine. Your path is different. Never let that heart close again. To love…that is your path. Do you not see how the situation you are in now is a blessing? Do you not see it? Heaven has given you the opportunity to live a life that is different than mine. Live a life with an open heart. Of course, living like that brings risks, the risk of getting hurt. But can't you see that to love like you love now is worth the risk? To feel love with this intensity your whole life is worth the risk.
I ran my fingers through Dad's salt-and-pepper hair.
Me: Your hair is still grey!
Daddy: My hands, my hair…this is the way you remember me. But up here I really don't look like this. Do you want to see what I really look like?
Me: Yes!
Suddenly, he transformed into light! Light with wings! He started flying away, but said one last thing to me. "Always live with an open heart, my beautiful daughter."
BOOM

When I returned from this travel, I just sat silently for a little while. Dad had come to me on multiple occasions before, but there were usually other souls around. Once before, he said, "I like it up here more than São Jorge!" That made me smile because my father loved his island more than almost anything in this world. But today, he came to me by himself and the power of this vision was almost overwhelming.

As my visions progressed, I learned an important truth about this universe and heaven. There is just love on the other side. There are no judgments, theology, dogmas, or any other rigid belief systems. Just love. Before I married, I often wondered if my father would have approved. He was a conservative thinker and we would find ourselves laughing sometimes at his possible reaction to my wedding, were he alive. Mama joked about it. "Your dad is probably rolling over in his grave right now!" Yet, what my travels were teaching me was that no such judgments exist on the other side.

Why do we spend so much time judging and excluding others? This was not the way of God for when I was Heaven, all I could feel was peace, joy and unconditional love. My sun—whom I came to understand was God—had always welcomed me with open arms. When I touched it, all I felt was love. God loves us all and there is nothing you can do to change that love. But it occurred to me that if everyone were to know that God is pure unconditional love, we would all be free to seek her without a middle man—or a religious structure to guide us. Now imagine that each one of us could connect to Source on our own. Religious dogma and the differences they create would cease to exist. Some religions make God seem judgmental and punishing; others create a mystique that is difficult to navigate without help.

As a teenager, I remembered many passages of the Bible from Sunday school. One of the most powerful was Jesus telling his disciples, "The kingdom of Heaven is within you." To my mind, He meant that if you wanted to find God, just close your eyes and look within. Imagine the impact His message had, especially in an age where high priests and

Pharisees stood as the sole channel between heaven and earth. In my short, but powerful travels, I learned so much about the other side and about myself. I finally understood why I had always been uncomfortable with the image of a white-bearded, fearful God. It never made sense that only some people were the "chosen ones" and everyone else went to hell. In fact, I was learning that hell didn't really exist at all. "Hell" is a mental construct that each one of us can create. Hell exists on earth, where egos help create our realities. Outside of the mind, there is no hell.

Initially, I didn't think much about the image of God I saw in my travels. It was a radiant sun, a perfect example of unconditional love. The sun shines equally on us all. No matter what your sins or salvations have been, the sun shines on you. The sun does not judge one to be unworthy and another to be good. Unconditional love, which brings us to God, just doesn't work like that. As I ascended, I felt that unconditional, judgment-free love. I truly understood that God had made me exactly the way I was. I also understood another one of Panache Desai's points when he said, "we are not broken and don't need fixing. We are perfect just the way we are." Indeed, the more I meditated and connected with the vast universe inside me, the more I understood the profound wisdom of these words. I was really beginning to love myself with a full heart and to understand life with an open heart.

Over time, I became adept at detecting when my ego was active. I could tell when my mind was interfering with the visualizations, because the images just didn't feel right. One lovely summer day, as I was meditating in Aunt Eva's Bay Area backyard, my mind interference was clear. I knew Jesus wasn't there. By now, I could rely on my feelings and energy more than the visual images, and I knew when my mind was forcing contact. These lessons were helping me to have more faith in what I was seeing. I was also starting to get proof from heaven.

My conversations with the other side continued to evolve rapidly while I was immersed in the wilderness of northern California. I had discovered a glorious park near where Aunt Eva lived, called Mount Madonna. I had never been immersed in a forest with redwoods of this size before. They looked like skyscrapers and had trunks the width of a bus. Walking under those trees was a humbling experience. Every time I touched one, I wondered just how much history she knew. How many generations of people had walked by her? I ran, hiked, and sprinted around the forest. But mostly, I spent my days here looking up at these gentle, massive giants.

Perhaps it was the communion with nature that helped elevate my energy frequency or perhaps I simply had a great master in JCS. During some daily meditation, my eyes would begin to tremble and I would hear his voice whisper, "Don't be afraid. Just let your body feel what it is going to feel right now." Suddenly, I would feel dizzy or a sense I was leaving my body. I would feel tingling or my heart rate would increase. I would remain calm and not ask too many questions. I couldn't explain what was happening to me and for the first time ever, I felt perfectly okay with that.

I can recall one travel during which JCS was particularly talkative. But there was something different. It was the first time he repeatedly emphasized a word: vortex. When he said the word—or rather when I felt it—I could tell he wanted me to remember it. I hadn't the slightest clue why, but would learn the answer a little later. What I did know was that there was more to this story. There was something missing here.

Two days later, I was volunteering at the famed Esalen Institute, in Big Sur. Esalen is well known in the spiritual community as a place of retreat, workshops, and rest and relaxation. It's perched on the hills overlooking the Pacific Ocean. Most of the great contemporary spiritual teachers have given workshops at Esalen and I felt a pull to be there. I had asked to volunteer in their farm and garden so I could get my hands dirty and experience its beauty. I had also signed up for a weekend "Soul-Centered Writing" workshop, being taught by the wonderful meditation teacher, Sarah McLean. At this point, the book Jesus wanted me to write was going nowhere and I felt that perhaps this workshop could help kick start the process. By now, I accepted that my soul wanted me to write a book. I wasn't just trying to do something Jesus had asked of me. I wanted to write this book for myself, as part of my path. It was the first time I truly felt the difference between what the mind wants and what the soul desires. When you find what the soul desires, you feel ecstatic! It feels like the action or work you are setting out to do is in your DNA.

Great. So…what next? I knew my soul wanted to write a book, but what would it be about? As soon as I asked myself this question, the answer popped up in my head. "I wish to write my story." Hmm. I spent most of my two hour drive to Big Sur thinking about this. And as usual, my ego was fast to judge. "Who would want to read about your life? That's dumb." But before I got caught up in the movies my mind was creating, I brought myself back to the present moment and noticed exactly where I was driving. I was going south on California Highway 1. It was breathtaking. Serpentine and flowing, the road unfolds along the ocean, overlooking vast stretches of blue sky, azure water and rugged cliff faces dropping down to the water.

By the time I entered Esalen, I already felt at peace. Being there was remarkably therapeutic. Seeing my hands working through the honest soil reminded me of my childhood and the joy I felt on our little farm. As I looked at my dirty hands, I was reminded of my father's and I went back to the good times I had experienced as a child. It wasn't all pain. Between gardening and my time hiking in northern California, I realized just how much I missed toiling in the earth and being outdoors communing with nature. It had been my therapy as a child and

I now understood deeply what the Azores had given me.

At the end of the two-day workshop, I felt completely different about the whole writing process. We spent the weekend in meditation, silence and free writing, as well as sharing our writing in the group. It was the free writing that helped the most. Free writing is the idea that I can just put my pencil on a piece of paper and write...without thinking or editing. Just write words fluidly as they form. I understood the difference between writing with your mind and writing with your soul. I decided to set myself some rules.

1. I would not to push myself if the words didn't come immediately.
2. I would meditate every day before starting.
3. I would write continuously without editing.

As an instructor, Sarah was generous, witty and wise. In those two days, she shared critical tips and insights into meditation, dispelling some common misunderstandings, such as the idea that to meditate effectively, you have to stop all thoughts. And, as it turned out, Sarah would also be the vehicle by which I received some "proof" from Heaven.

Towards the end of my stay, I bought one of her books and found her in the dining hall having lunch. I wanted her to sign it for me. She scribbled something inside and handed it back, smiling at me while she did. I thanked her and, not wanting to intrude on her personal time, headed over to a spot overlooking the ocean, where I could eat. Afterwards, I walked out to the lawn and sat on a bench by myself. I looked down at Sarah's book and finally decided to peek at what she had written. To my astonishment, her message read: "Tina, you are a vortex of delight! Keep meditating!" *Vortex*! The very word JCS had repeated over and over two days earlier. The hair on my body stood on end and I felt a powerful surge of joy rush through me. Jesus had sent me the proof I was asking for. It would be the first of many times Heaven spoke to me through life.

My life had undergone a radical change. I thought writing would be difficult. I had no idea where I would start. Yet one morning I just got up early, meditated for 20 minutes and then sat down at my iPad. I then took a deep breath and started typing without even realizing what I was saying. Einstein's quote about miracles came to my mind and then the words just started pouring out of me.

"When she was small, Christina Marie intuitively understood that everything was a miracle..."

Within ten days, I had written more than 50,000 words. With each sentence describing my early trauma and fears, I felt my soul growing lighter. Often, I felt astonishment at the level of detail and memory I had stored in my head. I didn't realize how therapeutic this process would be, how my soul yearned for a vehicle to process old pain and release it into the universe. With each passing day, I felt my energy rise.

There are so many lessons I learned over this intense period. One key concept related to time, or rather the limited way in which we view it. On the other side, time and distance are non-existent. They are merely a construct of the mind. For example, to you and me, 'soon' means that an event or moment is imminent. In Heaven, Jesus and others used the word, too, yet nothing seemed to change on earth. In Heaven, I realized that 'soon' could mean years, since our concept of time is linear and almost inflexible. It runs forward at the same pace, forever. In heaven, years can be just a blink of an eye since they view things with a grander perspective, sometimes over multiple lifetimes. "Soon" became one of those words I learned meant one thing to me and another to them.

Then there was the whole concept of destiny. I had come to

expect certain things to happen because I saw them in Heaven. If I could view future events, then maybe I could just sit back and wait for things to unfold. Yet like so much to do with human endeavor, destiny is fluid. We make and remake our futures with every decision taken, moment by moment. Your life isn't a pre-written script. Your intention and the energy that you emanate manifest in the physical form. And you can choose what materializes in your life. I could have chosen to continue emanating fear the day my wife left me. It was a conscious decision to change myself. The moment I did, my destiny changed, too.

27 PROOF FROM HEAVEN

My conversations with Jesus seemed to follow the same pattern. I would prepare myself with music and candles, then lie down with my eyes closed. But one day, I was meditating outside, sitting on the lawn of my aunt's beautifully manicured backyard, when I suddenly felt my eyes tremble. My 'antenna' was connected. "Father?" I said in my head. "I'm here my child. We have a lot to talk about." I have to admit, I hesitated. I'd never spoken to Him this way. I assumed it was my ego talking. I forced my attention back to my breathing. My eyes stopped trembling instantly. I continued my meditation session, then lay down on the cool grass and closed my eyes. I wanted to see if I had really been talking to Him. When I ascended and entered my field, Father was there waiting for me with His arms crossed.

06/19/13
Me: Sorry Father, but I was meditating and didn't trust it was really you talking to me.
Father: Well, that's what I wanted to talk about. From now on I may wish to speak to you at various times and you have to be prepared for that. I may wish to speak to you in the middle of a crowd, in an airport, or when you are driving somewhere. You no longer need a specific music or

routine to connect with me. You have to believe in yourself more.
Me: You really wanted to talk to me today?
Father: Yes! I wanted to tell you to stop wasting time on the internet looking for a job. I need your energy focused now on this book. This book is very important. From now on, you don't need to fight for anything. Let life bring you the experiences you need. Let the river take you to the right destination. Your times of struggle are over. When you surrendered yourself to me, everything changed. Trust me.
Suddenly, I was thinking about the little money I had in my bank account. Before I could ask Father about it, He was already answering.
Father: You're worried about the money. Don't ever focus on the lack of something but rather, focus always on the abundance that already exists inside you. Tell me, what is lacking in this precise moment?
Me: Nothing, Father.
Father: Exactly!
Father then walked away but turned around to say one last thing. "Don't worry about a job right now. Focus on your book."
BOOM

I had been spending a lot of time searching for work online. For weeks, no one called back or even acknowledged my applications. I had multiple degrees, I was highly qualified, so why wasn't I hearing from anyone? Fear started to creep into my thoughts. As my money dwindled and my student loans were about to fall due, I wanted to panic. Jesus wanted me to stop looking for jobs—was He kidding? This was probably the biggest test of my faith yet. Did I really trust my conversations with Jesus? Did I trust Jesus Himself? I was struggling to let life unfold without a fight. I knew that fighting for things meant the soul didn't want what the mind wanted. But surely one has to actually apply for a job in order to get one? How could I survive by just writing the book and hoping life would plop something great on my doorstep? In the end, I decided to trust in faith. Following my ego's direction hadn't worked out so well, so perhaps faith and blind hope would.

06/21/13

I was meditating outside, when my eyes started trembling again. I felt the word 'ascend', so I did. I was in my field, but I couldn't see very well. It was unsettling.

Me: Father, I don't trust these conversations very much, because I cannot see you. Please send me a sign so I can be sure.

Father: I will. Now, stop focusing on my image and focus instead on my voice.

Suddenly, I heard sounds everywhere! The neighbor turned on her music really loud and the gardeners started mowing the lawn with super loud machines! There was noise everywhere!

Father: Are you listening to all this noise? This is a practice. You have to learn how to listen to me in the middle of chaos. Sometimes, life may seem like a chaos because the Universe is always moving, always expanding. But life is not a chaos in the negative sense—it's a blessed chaos. And I need you to learn how to listen to me in this chaos. Your life is going to move very quickly now. You can't live in this peace and quiet your whole life. These trees, the birds, nature, this was a gift from heaven. It was a gift so you could center yourself, center your heart. But now you will move. And I need you to hear me in the chaos of life. Concentrate on my voice. Concentrate on the thoughts that enter your mind from above. It is me talking to you.

BOOM

I was so excited when I opened my eyes. This was the first real conversation I had with Jesus outside of my regular travels. I was just sitting outside meditating when my antenna connected. Was this the way He wanted to talk to me from now on? I went back over our conversation in my mind and one word kept coming up: chaos.

I wandered over to my aunt's heavy wooden dining room table to start my writing for the day. I grabbed my journal and flipped it open, randomly stopping at a note I had written to Catherine in 2011. Odd. And there it was, a sign. I had written, "but know that regardless of all the chaos there is one constant: my love for you. Always." BOOM! Heaven really was amazing. I was learning that Heaven speaks to us constantly, if we only listen. Heaven speaks to us through life and many times, through messages so subtle we miss them completely, especially when we're immersed in the daily melodrama our minds create. If we live too much in the past or in the future, we miss so many messages from Heaven. Too often, we wander from point A to point B on autopilot, missing the little cues life is giving us. This is one of the main reasons why living intensely in the present moment is so important. In every single moment, in the present, Heaven speaks to you. As you will soon realize, the day you focus on the now is the day you will hear life's messages more clearly.

06/22/13

I was meditating outside again and my eyes began trembling. I knew my antenna was connected.

Father: Hello, my treasure!

Me: Hi Father! Thanks for the sign yesterday!

Father: Yes, it was cool right?

Me: Yes! Father, yesterday I didn't feel very well. My body sometimes feels ill.

Father: My treasure, I know your body feels ill sometimes, but don't panic. Don't be afraid. Just let your body feel whatever it feels. Don't judge your body. You have always been this way—sensitive to the energies of the universe. You know, there's a lot you don't know or need to know. Know only that there are energies in the universe and your body can feel them. Your heart chakra has a door that is thinner than most. It's like a screen door that allows wind in and out. The majority of people down there have a glass door on their heart chakra. But a screen door is permeable. And that is the way your body is. The heart chakra is the door to the inner world—where energy is infinite. There are things that grab your heart chakra because the door is thin and so your internal light is always visible. Denser energies are attracted to light. Do you understand? When these energies get close to your heart chakra, you can feel it. I need for you to understand that God made your body this way for a reason. You function as one of my hands on earth. Through you I can work down there. You have always been a healer, my treasure. But now you will help others through your energy. Your job now down there is an energetic one. I need

*your antenna to always be on, my treasure. It is through bodies like yours
that Heaven descends to Earth. Do you understand? There's a group of
you down there who are helping the world increase in energy frequency. I
descend to earth through you all and work like a…vacuum cleaner.
Through you, I descend and suck up all the dirt that is on earth. The
more I vacuum, the more the earth's energy will increase. I know it's not
easy feeling how you feel sometimes. I know you feel ill at times and that
causes fear in you. My treasure, when you begin to feel ill—when your
body senses that something is wrong—all you have to do is call for me and
I will vacuum it all. Don't panic or try to know why you are feeling a
particular way. There is much you do not know about the universe, so
don't waste time wanting to know everything. Just remember to call for me.
You know, your beautiful grandmother used to feel the same way. There's
nothing wrong with how your body perceives the world. So just call for me
and wait patiently for the illness to leave you. Without fear. Okay, go
write down what I just said because I spoke a lot today.*
*Me: Father, you have never called me your treasure before. Are you
repeating the word because you're going to send me another sign?*
I could feel him smiling.
Father: Maybe, my TREASURE.
BOOM

I rushed into the house so I could transcribe everything He
had said today. He had never talked that much before. I'm
pretty sure my transcription left some things out, but I would
learn to feel and remember the most important things Jesus
said to me. On this day, He focused on 'treasure.' I want to say
that Jesus 'speaks' to me in Portuguese—I have no idea why.
Then again, so does my Vó and Dad.

When I finished transcribing my conversation, I got up and
decided the living room needed cleaning, so I grabbed the
vacuum cleaner (ironic isn't it?). Suddenly, a big picture frame
holding a photo of my grandparents fell face down. As I
picked it up, I discovered it had landed on a book written by
my great grandfather about the island of São Jorge. I smiled to
myself. That the picture frame could not have possibly fallen

by itself. I just felt it. I inspected the outside of the book, but didn't see the word 'treasure' anywhere. Nothing on the first few pages, either. Huh. Maybe I was wrong to assume this was the work of Father. And then I heard it, a tiny whisper urging me to flip the page. And there it was. My great grandfather had written that São Jorge possessed "...treasures of a strong nature, sometimes aggressive, sometimes soft and sometimes full of surprises." BOOM! My hands shook a little. In the past, I usually stumbled upon signs Jesus sent me. But today was different. It was as if a poltergeist had flipped the photo off the wall. Holding the book, I lowered myself onto the couch and closed my eyes. I thanked Jesus for this thunderous sign, smiling as I did so. It may be that faith shouldn't require proof, but I welcomed the signs nonetheless.

During our conversation, I had asked Him about my body. My feelings still caused a rush of cortisone, the 'fight or flight' hormone. Some days, I would wake up feeling as if there was an extra body slung across on my shoulders. I'd struggle to breathe. On other days, I'd feel great, only to have a sudden heaviness overcome me. If someone close to me was ill, I'd feel it physically. Then, there were the panic attacks in the middle of the night. Rapid heart rate, hyperventilation, the feeling someone else was inside my brain.

But according to Jesus, this was how my body worked and I needed to get used to it. The next night, I would get an opportunity to practice He preached. I was sleeping and awoke in a panic, as I had done frequently since my teenage years. Disoriented, I sat bolt upright and called for Jesus. "Father, please help me." In an instant, it was gone—the panic, the pressure, the anxiety had vanished. My heart rate dropped, my respiration slowed and I could think normally. In the past, my panic attacks would take 15 minutes to normalize, using sheer willpower. But this was different. I didn't do anything except call for Father. And just like that it was gone.

I was learning so much about myself and the nature of my panic attacks. The anxiety I experienced most of life could not explained through simple biochemistry. It could not be cured or managed with drugs and traditional psychotherapy, as the source was spiritual in nature. In the past, I had used breathing techniques and even drugs to help manage my anxiety. Yet they would not cure my anxiety because I had to go much deeper to find the source of my panic attacks. Now that I was connecting with my true nature, I discovered the root of the problem was spiritual and it was being healed every single time I connected with the other side. I was learning that my nature, that of a healer, could only really come through when I healed myself first.

06/26/13

JCS: You have always been a healer and always wanted to carry everyone else's pain. But do you know that even in that respect you were just trying to derive a better sense of worth from the outside world? You wanted to carry others' pain because it increased your self-esteem. But as you know, your work will be energetic. And that means you must now learn to just BE with someone else's pain. You have to learn how to bear witness to someone else's pain, without wanting to take it away. You must learn to put your hand on another's and simply say: "I am here for you."
BOOM

28 DROPPING ATTACHMENTS

07/03/13
Father: Hello, my beautiful daughter!
Me: Father, I've felt very unsettled lately.
Father: I know, child. Meditation is key. Do you know that you can meditate anywhere...even in the middle of a rock concert! Meditation is about exploring your inner world, the infinite universe within. You will learn soon enough. Your book is almost finished! It's almost time.
Me: How will I know I've reached the end?
Father: You will. Your soul will know! It's almost time for people to know about our relationship.
BOOM

Meditation. It seemed to be the key to my spiritual evolution, but I felt like such a novice. I had always read that meditation needed to be performed in a certain way, yet Jesus told me I could meditate in the middle of a concert. I was confused. To me, meditation meant sitting quietly and focusing on my breath. I had made a habit of opening my session up by ringing a Tibetan singing bowl. That melodic humming enters my core and triggers something. I'd close my eyes and scan my body, ensuring I relaxed from head to toe. Then, I'd focus on my breathing, or sometimes on parts of my body. If a thought floated to the surface, I'd gently say the word 'thinking' in my mind. This mantra, or the use of targeted words to bring your focus back to the present moment, had been recommended by renowned Buddhist teacher, Pema Chodron. Some meditation teachers do not like to label thoughts when they emerge. For me, the word 'thinking' refocused my attention.

Meditation is a perfect vehicle by which to practice kindness toward yourself. By drawing yourself gently back when you have wandering thoughts, you have the opportunity to be kind to yourself. No judgment, no harsh reminders. Sometimes, I'd even smile when a thought came to me. Initially, I would feel irritated and fidget when a thought came. I'd get up in anger and pace before sitting back down. Each time I felt that annoyance, I would take a deep breath and just think, "It's okay." With each session, I started to love myself more than I thought was possible.

07/03/13
Me: You told me I was going to stop suffering soon.
Father: Have you noticed that you are waiting for a certain person to come back before you stop suffering? You just wrote a wedding sermon for your friends in which you talk about how people need to be complete in themselves before they walk into a marriage. You said people had to love from an overflowing cup…that the full cup represented self-love and the overflow was love of others. You said people can't really love another until they love themselves. Yet it seems this is another example of you writing beautiful words, then not living those words in your own life. You don't need anyone in order to stop suffering. You must learn how to live what you write my child. Has it ever occurred to you that I want you to live without attachment? That is all I want you to lose: attachment. I want you to love without attachment.
BOOM

Yes, I was waiting for a certain someone to come back to me before I stopped suffering. And yes, I had written a beautiful wedding sermon for my friends Kim and Courtney, in which I planned to share with their friends and family how we needed to be complete in ourselves before we enter a marriage. I suppose part of me understood those words because I hadn't lived them, but knew that's where I wanted to be.

But marriage is just one social contract we undertake. What about the bigger picture, in which each individual—whether they marry or not, whether they live alone or not—should be the whole version of themselves? And how do we get there? It made me wonder about the 'stuff' we have around us and the people we have in our lives who keep us distracted and busy. If we lost all of it—the friends, the family, the house, the car— would we be happy? Most people would answer no. Most of us believe we need something outside of us in order to be happy. Our partners, families, friends, jobs, achievements, holidays and gadgets are all badges of happy achievement. And yet, I was starting to realize just how precarious such tenuous attachments are, when it comes to our happiness. If your partner makes you happy, he or she can also make you unhappy. Every time you assign that power to someone or something, you give away your self-direction, you rely on someone else to complete your happiness.

When you give someone else the power to keep or make you happy, you put a burden on them. Your partner or friend must live his or her life in a conforming way so as to not disturb your happiness. But in order to conform to your happiness, your spouse must give up a little bit of himself. Think about this. You have required another person to live in a constraining way just so you could be happy. You have asked them to forsake themselves in order to keep your internal world intact. Would you be happy knowing that?

The alternative is simple: don't need. Don't give anyone the power to make you anything—not even your soul mate. When you realize that your soul wants to stand independently, you will find the power of inner abundance. When you take a deep breath and realize that happiness and joy is already within you, your life will change. Not only will you become fully centered in yourself, but you'll realize the huge burden you take off those who surround you. Your partner will live his or her life in freedom—the freedom to be who they are and not who they need to be for your happiness. Only then will you find unconditional love.

This is love—letting the object of your affections be no one but who they are. If you continue to rely on your spouse to make you happy, you will never get to know them. As Jesuit priest and spiritual teacher Anthony de Mello said in *The Way to Love*, "You cannot love what you do not even see." You will never let the real them see the light of day. If you want to love people for exactly who they are, close your eyes and see the abundance already in you. Of course, your partner or family members add to your happiness. They just shouldn't be given the responsibility to make you happy.

07/04/13
Me: I feel a bit depressed. I'm not sure why.
Father: Don't be so hard on yourself. Be kind to yourself. You know, the other day I said you needed to learn how to just be with someone else's pain. But I want you to learn that lesson for yourself, too. In truth, we cannot put forth into this world anything we do not have for ourselves. So learn to just be with your own pain. Put your hand on your chest and say, 'I am here for you.' When you start to feel a little down, ask yourself, 'What is lacking in this precise moment?' You will find that nothing is ever lacking in the present moment. I also want you to learn how to stand on your own two feet, without needing anything in your external world to help complete you. I want you to learn how to be with the abundance that you already have inside and not rely on the outside to help keep you standing. This is the only way you receive the infinite love heaven has to give. I want you to learn that you need nothing in order to be happy. Nothing and no one.
BOOM

It seemed clear at this point that JCS was really focusing on living without attachment. Well, alright, then. It was important to learn this. But how? The first step seemed to be that I should identify the things and people to whom I was attached: my ex-wife, the initials after my name, my intellect. Check. But how does one drop these attachments?

> "…the process is not painful at all. On the contrary, getting rid of attachments is a perfectly delightful task if the instrument you use to rid yourself of them is not willpower or renunciation but sight. All you need to do is open your eyes and see that you do not really need the object of your attachment at all." ~ Anthony de Mello

Ah. So simple, so true. Rather than renouncing an attachment—and thereby focusing all your energy on it—simply let it go. If you say to yourself "stop thinking of my ex", your mind focuses on your ex. Renunciation never works. What works is sight and awareness. I realize that sounds rather vague, but by becoming aware of your attachments, you can leave them behind. When you clearly see that you are attached to something or someone, you begin to realize that you do not need that someone or something in order to happy or fulfilled. An attachment is really only created when you think you need something. In my life, I used my intellect and romantic relationships to increase my self-worth. These attachments had formed because I did not know how to love or respect myself, so I tried to acquire those feelings from my outside environment. This brings me back to processing emotions. Letting emotions process is a one-step deal. You become aware of the emotions and they slowly fade. And here I was learning that the same process applied to attachments. Sometimes, the universe is brilliant in its simplicity.

When I flew to New York City to perform Kim and Courtney's wedding, my mind was mulling over this whole idea of dropping attachments. The one-step approach applied to everything except for my ex-wife. I struggled to drop the 'need' from my attachment. The process itself may be simple, but executing it was harder than I realized, because I was also dealing with the pain of loss.

07/05/13
Me: I'm trying to shed my attachments but it's hard. How do I learn to live without attachment?
Father: Meditation, self-love, kindness towards yourself. When you realize just how abundant you are inside, you will cease to need anything on the outside. Do you really know what lies within you? Do you know the abundance that is inside you? Explore that more. Find your inner abundance and all needs will drop.
BOOM

I was beginning to love myself and I was using constant acts of kindness to build that self-love. But perhaps He was right: I was still only scratching the surface. We live in a society where worth is externalized. Most of us rarely take the time to discover what lies within. It seems like such an outré concept— accessible only to Zen masters or yogis.

But let's take a step back at this point. What does 'acts of kindness' mean? Does it mean booking a vacation to Australia, financed by the bank? Does it mean indulging in a week-long marathon of Audrey Hepburn films in front of the TV? Does it mean telling yourself it's okay to buy another pair of shoes, suit or expensive tie, because you deserve it, dammit? You know what I'm going to say next. Treating yourself can be good R & R for the soul, provided you realize that the word 'treat' refers to a once-in-a-while incident. But true self-kindness doesn't stem from sitting on a beach for a week. Sure, you have the photos and the tan (at least for a few weeks), but unless you deal with it, you carry your prison cell anywhere you go.

What I mean by 'acts of kindness' is something so radically simple, it can be hard to comprehend. It could mean dropping the illusion of perfection. It could mean saying 'It's okay' when you're hurt. Most acts of self-kindness spring from the realization that you are good enough just the way you are. Back to Panache Desai's words: "You are not broken, and don't need fixing." And yet, as humans, we constantly strive for perfection. What is perfection and how can we ever attain it? We can't. Think about it. We are all glorious, hilarious, gorgeous hot messes. But when we try to tack on 'perfectionist' to our hot mess, we only increase our egos. That's because like 'infinity', perfection is a mathematic impossibility. So let it go. Just. Let. It. Go. Accept that you'll make mistakes, get hurt, create hurt, screw up. It's okay. God loves you as you are, you gorgeous, hot mess.

29 A CENTRAL PARK WEDDING

Back in New York, I had fun. I saw many old friends, met some new ones and the wedding went off without a hitch. It was a hot, gorgeous New York City day. As a trumpeter and vocalist sang The Temptations' hit, 'My Girl', while Kim and Courtney walked across the lawn escorted by their parents, random dog walkers broke into spontaneous applause. The joy amongst us was palpable. And yet…yes, my ex-wife was there. I was at center stage, saying those words, while Catherine looked on. It was both painful and wonderful. She was wearing a deep pink dress and simple jewelry. Her hair was perfectly straight and blown out—a routine she repeated every time she dressed up and went out. It was excruciatingly difficult to remain somewhat unaffected, while simultaneously greeting guests as they arrived. *Keep it together.* I was marrying two close friends and the thought of messing up their perfect day with my own drama was causing a bit of anxiety. *Keep it together.* My friend Moni noticed I may be in need of some emotional support. "What a beautiful day for a wedding!" Her perfectly timed comment broke me out of my mental turmoil. I smiled as I looked at her. "Yes it is."

As Moni and I made small talk, Catherine came over to say

hello. When I embraced her, I felt just how much I had missed her. I also felt the intensity of my love for her. She was so beautiful, so unattainable, I suppose. Back in New York, where I had spent so much of my life, I guess my mind idly reminisced and dawdled over what had been, what she said and what I said, or should have. I replayed the conversation over and over until it was perfect—in retrospect. I was sure that she could feel my love, could see how much I had learned and how much better things could be. A few minutes later, someone nudged me. The brides had arrived. It was time to marry them. As they walked slowly toward me across the lawn, I felt my heart exploding with happiness. I could feel their deep love for each other and the joy in their hearts that this day was finally here. As they reached me, we just stood there for a few minutes smiling at each other. We were just basking in the beautiful energy all around us.

As I lifted my eyes to the crowd ahead and prepared to start the ceremony, my eyes met Catherine's as she was standing close to the front of the pack. *Keep it together.* I felt a momentary spark of fear in my stomach. *I can't concentrate on what I have to say while she's staring at me.* In that very moment, one of the wedding guests slipped right in front of her and eye contact was broken. I swallowed and started to speak. "I wanted to start off this wonderful ceremony by welcoming everyone and thanking you all for being here today..."

A few days later, I was back in northern California, returning to my transient life. I walked into the house, plopped down my luggage and opened my computer. Catherine had sent me an email. I was so eager to open it, I could feel my pulse skip.

She wanted to move ahead with the divorce. My mouth went dry. But then, something happened. I paused. "Good try, little devil," I thought to myself. I took a deep breath, relaxed my body and reread the email. Tears flowed. I cried for a few moments. The knot in my stomach dissipated. I said aloud, "I accept whatever life brings me. Even this." When you live with an open heart, emotions pass through you quickly and you suffer less. If she really wanted to move forward with a divorce, then I was absolutely going to accept her decision. This was yet another lesson on how to love unconditionally. I sat with my pain for a little while, and then went to meditate before having another conversation with JCS.

07/10/13

Me: Father, are you there?

Father: I'm always here my child.

Me: I accept what you are sending me. I don't always know why you send certain things but I accept what is coming my way.

Father: I'm very proud of you. You are truly learning to love unconditionally. You know, what others do or say is none of your business. What is your business is how you respond to people and to all the events that life sends your way. You are each responsible for how you interact with the world. I am sending you gifts, my pearl. They may not feel like gifts to you now, but they are. You cannot teach others how to tame their egos if you do not first tame yours. A real teacher is one who teaches from experience, not theories. The world is filled with theories. But an authentic teacher is one that has walked over the hot coals before she teaches someone else how to do it. Don't you see that you cannot do the spiritual work that is part of your path until you learn how to love unconditionally? That is the ultimate lesson for those that follow a spiritual path. You are learning to love C down there as you do up here, in Heaven. And that makes me so very happy.

BOOM

Yes, the "gifts" life was sending me didn't feel like gifts at the time, but I was absolutely certain they were just as priceless as the happiest moments of my life. Life is made up of duality, the yin and yang, the good and bad, the highs and the lows. You cannot know what happiness is unless you experience unhappiness. Light would mean nothing without darkness; the same for cold without hot. We shouldn't want to escape such duality, because it is within those contrasts that we find the richness of life, the lessons to be learned and pleasure of experiencing everything fully. As an Australian friend of mine puts it, "You have to take the crunchy with the smooth." When you embrace the transition from unhappiness, for example, you can feel a depth of joy much profoundly than before. So why do we close our hearts and resist when life sends us some painful moments? Really, it's not worth it to resist because you will only suffer more. But not only that, why would you resist something that is here to teach you "perspective"?

07/12/13
Me: Hello Father! I can tell you are happy today!
Father: It makes me happy that you are learning all the lessons I am sending. You are also learning to understand me without words. I do not need to speak for you to feel my truth.
Me: What about a job father?
Father: You know the answer to that, my child. Your soul has been answering you for a while now. Are you listening to it? Today, your soul said, 'I want to write.' Did you hear it? Writing shall be a very important part of your path now, my pearl.
Me: But how can I make a living...
Father: There is no need to finish that question, for you know the answer already. You have been writing about allowing your soul to command, not your mind. Well, live this truth my child. You need not worry about a thing when you listen to your soul; when you give it freedom to be what it wants in this life. Remember the dam example you gave in your book? That is exactly what happens when you break the grip of the ego: your dam cracks. When a dam breaks it brings with it an abundance of water that flows out like a raging river. The same happens when your soul is heard. When your soul breaks through the grip of the ego, it brings with it an abundance that you cannot even grasp. You need not worry about making a living in your next job for you will have abundance.
BOOM

I was slowly learning to feel what JCS was communicating

to me without words. On this day, I could tell He was happy even before He started talking to me. I could feel He had a smile on his face even though I could not see Him. And yes, my soul had indeed been answering me for some time now, but today, I got more detailed information than I had before. I had made a habit of asking three questions during my daily meditation sessions and one of them—What does my soul desire? — had been yielding some interesting answers. I knew my soul wanted to teach, to share my spiritual journey with others and help them awaken. The idea of becoming a motivational speaker had come to me after one of my meditations. But I had no idea how I was going to transition from being a clinician to a spiritual teacher. My ego would sometimes chime in and laugh at me for even considering this as my next big career move. Fortunately, the little devil on my shoulder was being completely ignored these days. His voice had quieted down substantially with my daily meditation practice and when he did whisper in my ear, I just said, "Thank you for your opinion."

But now, when I had asked my soul what it desired, I got an immediate response: "I want to write." I instantly thought of New York, where so many people dream of becoming actors, but then end up bartending to make ends meet. How could I ever make a living writing? Yet, JCS was again reminding me that I need not worry about the road ahead once I decide to let my soul command. This was all new and so I will concede that my internal barometer felt discomfort with the idea of writing as a full-time job. But he was giving me more details than he had before. "Writing shall be a very important part of your path now, my pearl." Okay, at least I was getting warmer when it came to my next career move!

This whole conversation with JCS also reminded me how much I had changed. I was now at a place where all this uncertainty was welcomed. I actually felt peace and calm. I felt excited about what lie ahead, even if I had no idea what that was. It was as if I had experienced death and come back a whole new person. In this case, it was the death of fear, anxiety, worry, loneliness. You might be thinking: "How do you not feel lonely if your wife left you?" Well, perhaps I really was dropping my attachment to her. But it was more than that, I now loved myself. And as spiritual teacher Wayne Dyer once said, "You cannot be lonely if you like the person you're alone with." I not only liked the person I was alone with...I loved her. I was feeling what JCS meant by "inner abundance" and it was amazing.

07/20/13

Me: Father, my eyes are shaking a lot today. Do you want to speak to me?

He did not respond, but I could again feel He was happy and smiling.

Father: Sometimes, I just want to be connected with you so that I can share my energy. We don't always have to talk. I am giving you my energy. We sat in silence for a while and I could again tell He was smiling.

Father: You know, up until now, we have focused a lot on your transformation. We have focused on you and your life. But from now on, we will move to other projects. Your life is going to profoundly change. Do you feel that yet?

Me: Yes, I can feel that something is going to change. I'm just not sure what.

Father: Well, in all honesty so much has already changed. You have transformed and that makes me so happy. But now your path is going to be different. Remember when I said you were like my hand, helping me descend and work on Earth? I said that I worked like a vacuum cleaner? Well, you are also going to be my hand for something else. I have a lot to share with humanity and you will be my hand and write it all down. Listen, the Earth's energy is changing. It is increasing and with it, so too must your level of consciousness. You will help me disseminate my messages to others. This book you are now writing...it is the first of many. Don't focus too much on imagining the future. Continue living intensely in the present moment and you will see how this all turns out. Now, you will finish this book. Then...more will come.

BOOM

JCS seemed to be making clear that he was going to work with me directly in this new phase of my life. And I welcomed that. I also began to feel what He meant by disseminating his messages to others. I wasn't suddenly going to write a new Bible or some other religious text. Rather, it would be energetic. I wasn't going to tell people how to connect and listen to ascended masters (like Jesus, Archangel Michael or Buddha to name a few), I was going to show people how to do it. In truth, one of the main focuses of my teachings would be on showing others that we are all "prophets" and can all connect to Jesus or any other ascended master. Connection to other realms was what I would teach.

30 LIVING IN THE PRESENT MOMENT

Hearing about my future books didn't surprise me much since I already knew writing was going to be a significant part of my path now. But this conversation with JCS felt different. It felt like I had somehow reached a goal he had set for me and he was telling me what would happen next. Before, he guided me in my own transformation, but now he seemed to open another door. I would now take my lessons and his messages, and disseminate them. But there was still one repeating theme: living in the present moment. Of all the many lessons I had learned, none seemed as important as living in the now. Sometimes, living in the present moment can seem esoteric. What does this even mean? Aren't we always present in the present? What it means is that you live every moment as if it were your last. Now, before you go grab your bucket list from the drawer, we're not talking about skydiving or jumping off a cliff. My bucket list starts with "Dive with great white sharks." And one day, I hope to scratch that off my list. But a bucket list is not living in the present moment—it's something that you want to do in the future before you die. In truth, keeping a list of things you want to do before you die is far from living in the present. But what if you discovered you had just one hour to live? What would you do with those 60 minutes? I can tell you, it would force you to have laser focus on the present. Having that little time left would mean you would have to shed every single external thing in your environment in lieu of the now.

Even at its best and most sane, the world is a turbulent place filled with uncertainties and improbabilities. You know the stories I'm talking about, in which the cancer patient successfully fights off the disease, only to be hit by a bus on the way to his checkup. Try as we might to order the world to be predictable, life will always stick its foot out to trip you on your way out the door. Perhaps that's why the 'sudden death', the random accident or the 'senseless act of violence' rattles us so much. We are forced to face the reality that we can't control. So if you knew you had 60 minutes left, chances are you'd panic and then maybe focus on what you have left and act accordingly. But shouldn't we always live like that, as if every moment were potentially our last?

Of course, there's another valuable lesson to be learned here. If we had a choice, we'd probably want our last moments to be elegant, quiet, in our sleep and without pain. Or maybe, we'd like those last moments to be memorable, such as Oscar Wilde's famous last one-liner: "Either this wallpaper goes, or I do." But life—and death—just aren't like that. In Britain, the Queen Mother twice nearly had the inglorious fate of choking to death on fish bones when she was in her '80s. (She died in 2002 at 101, having also survived breast and colon cancer, a hip replacement, lesions on her legs and cataracts.) The point is that when people die odd deaths, we realize none of us are immune from life playing a joke by saying, "You think you're so important, but you just died by choking on a carrot! Ha!" If we're aware of it, death has the power to teach us humility because it can be unexpected and ridiculous, and it eventually happens to everyone, from you to the Queen Mother. So next time you hear someone talk about death as if it were a bad thing, remember that it is your greatest teacher. When you are immersed in your mental melodramas, remember how tenuous and fleeting life can be. This affirmation can immediately bring you back to the present moment—the only place where life actually unfolds.

31 FALLING IN LOVE AGAIN

In late July, I found myself on a plane bound for Portugal. Going home always filled my heart with joy, but this trip felt different. I was now looking at the world with completely new eyes and being home cemented that realization in me. One of the most remarkable things about developing self-love and self-compassion is that we then begin to transform everything around us. The spiritual and emotional work I had done in the previous months was now bearing fruit. I could look clearly at my own ego, which allowed me to also see everyone else's. Before, I would judge people based on what their little devils brought into this world. Now I found myself seeing their pain. I found myself looking at people's souls. This new development was most pronounced with my family, especially my mother. I could look at her and all of her complexities, and love her for exactly who she was. She didn't need to change or be anything other than who she was. I simply loved her. The same occurred with other people around me. I found myself loving people I didn't even think I liked. I could very clearly look at someone and completely acknowledge their humanity, their weaknesses, their egos, their strengths.

We so frequently think of peace as only being possible

when someone else changes. Peace talks seem to mean "you give up this and I give up this and we all live happily ever after." But true peace starts when we accept the responsibility of self-transformation. Quite simply, if you work on your inner environment, everything else will fall into place. Being home put me in contact with people from my past, some of whom I used to resent for things said or done. Yet the resentment was simply gone. In its place was a deep recognition that all humans have one thing in common: we are all gorgeous, hot messes! But seriously, consider it this way. If everyone decided to redirect their gaze inward, there wouldn't be as many dramas as there are in this world. Unfortunately, it is always easier to be self-righteous and demand that someone else change, rather than take on the challenge ourselves. By insisting on change in others, we neglect the joy that comes from self-transformation.

Joy, an emotion so very few of us allow to flow through our beings, was now a constant in me. I hadn't actually realized that my inner world was pulsating with joy until one day, while sitting outside and sipping coffee, it just hit me! Sure, I was jobless, with bills coming due and so much personal loss over the previous year. Yet it dawned on me that I was happier than I had ever been. It didn't matter what my life looked like from the outside. Inside, I felt whole and just knew that this time, I had found myself and what I was meant to do. I had no idea how I was going to get there, but it didn't matter. The joy in me would lead the way.

08/21/13
Me: Father, my life is taking rather unexpected turns.
Father: You are in a state of metamorphosis. Trust me. Your metamorphosis is going just as planned.
BOOM

Ah yes, the unexpected turns. Just like a bomb...BOOM...I fell in love with a beautiful, incredible being while I was back home on the island of my youth. It all happened when Kim and Courtney came to the island for their honeymoon. I was so happy with their arrival because it was the culmination of the celebration of their love. It brought such joy to my heart to marry them and it was a thrill to host them on their honeymoon. In the midst of our fun adventures and laughs at home with Mama, we went on a hike and returned a bit broken. I got sand in my eye and scratched it; Courtney struggled with what appeared to be a respiratory infection. "We're total messes!" We laughed in the kitchen after our hike. "You should go see my new doctor," said Mama. "She's working in the ER today so just stop by." I had heard my mom talk about her new family doctor, who had arrived on the island a few months before. I decided this was a good time to see what all the fuss was about.

When Courtney and I entered the ER, we were laughing and joking around. Then, Mom's doctor came into sight. "Whoa, she's hot," was the first thing I thought. By the time I entered her office and she got close to check my eye, another thought popped into my mind, "You're in trouble, Tina." I was immediately and intensely attracted to this woman. But I was also aware that my heart had been broken just a few months before. I had been resisting my mind's strong impulse to seek out romance and sex since my ex had left me. Then there were my friends. "You just need to get laid," they'd laugh. But my essence knew otherwise. I had done this before and it hadn't helped. My memory took me back to the months immediately after Melanie broke up with me. I felt the pain of those months resurface. I saw myself going from bar to bar—taking girls home, then forgetting about them a few days later. "I don't want to use sex as medicine ever again," I thought.

I was aware of how I let my sexual impulses dominate me in the immediate aftermath of my relationship with Melanie. With every sexual encounter, I felt worse. I was using sex as a way to feel desired again but afterwards, I felt like I was digging a deeper emotional hole for myself. Not only that, but when we use sex to sooth our internal pain, we rarely think what that might do to the partners we welcome into our beds. We are harming not only ourselves, but others too. I didn't want to do that anymore. I felt deeply that resisting my sexual impulses in the months after the breakup of my marriage turned out to be the best thing I could have done.

But here I was, intensely attracted to someone new. "What is this," I thought one day while meditating. My mind followed up with some internal dialogue. "It doesn't matter. She's probably straight, so don't even go there." A few days later, I went with some friends to an outdoor party and there she was. Susana* was with a guy who was visiting her from home, in mainland Portugal. He sent a nod in my direction and I smiled back. A few minutes later, on my way to the bathroom, I spotted him again, sitting on a couch. I decided to say hello. "You look bored," I said, as he looked at his cellphone. "Not at all! I'm just resting my legs. How are you? My name is Paul*!" After a few pleasantries, I saw Susana briskly walking in our direction. "Hello again! How's your eye?" I smiled. "It's doing much better, doctor, thanks." She immediately interrupted. "Please don't call me that. My name is Susana." Seeing her in plain clothes instead of scrubs brought out her beauty even more. She was in her early 30's, with dark long hair, olive skin, and deep brown eyes. Her gaze made my knees shake. She suddenly interrupted my thoughts. "You know, my friend here saw you walking by the other day and really liked you. He thinks you're the prettiest girl on this island…and I agree!" I immediately felt my body temperature increase. "She thinks I'm pretty!" But then my mind brought me back to Paul and his attraction to me. He was adorable and I sensed his energy deeply. He was a kind and gentle man, so I wanted to make sure I let him down gently. "Thank you for the compliment. But, well, I'm the island lesbian." I had used that line for a while and it always got a laugh. "That breaks my heart a little," Paul replied with a smile. Then, Susana hit me with another line that brought my body temperature up another notch. "Oh yeah? Well, I'm bi." My mind immediately started rumbling. "You're really in trouble now, Tina."

Fast forward a few days and I found myself at a dinner party at Susana's place. She and Paul had invited me after we exchanged numbers. I was nervous. I was so intensely attracted to this woman, I felt like a high school kid. But my soul whispered softly, "this is more than a physical attraction." As the night progressed, things started to get a little hot. Susana was most certainly flirting with me, but my little devil was rearing his head again. "Don't go there sister, she's going to reject you." Maybe the little bastard was right. I kept the internal dialogue going for a while as I helped clean the kitchen. Susana came over. "You're awfully quiet right now. What are you thinking about?" I looked straight into her eyes and responded without hesitation. "I'm thinking about how glad I am to be leaving back to the US next week. If I stayed here close to you much longer, I'd be in deep trouble." She immediately blushed and smiled. As she walked back toward her party guests, I was left with my damn devil. "You idiot! Why did you say that to her? You're setting yourself up for rejection." But just as my mind finished saying the word "rejection," something else in me spoke loudly.

I calmly put the dish I was washing down and walked over to Susana, in the dining room. I gently caught her hand and guided her to the next room. Once there, I didn't say a single word. I just pulled her body close to mine and kissed her. Just like that. BOOM. She initially pulled away from me. "What are you doing? Are you crazy? There are people in the other room!" But I didn't pay much attention to her weak protests and kissed her again.

I drove home in the wee hours of the morning, with a huge smile on my face. The devil was whispering again about the possibility of rejection, but I kept smiling. Sure, I was following my heart and that may lead to roads unchartered. But I was happy. I didn't know what tomorrow would bring and that was okay, too. I was determined to continue living with an open heart and it was telling me at this exact moment that Susana was not simply a summer fling. Whatever this was, it had to be pursued. End of story.

Our souls are love, one little piece of the infinite love that is Source or God. Our souls want to live openly and be exposed to all that life brings us because the soul knows no fear. It welcomes all that life brings. Is it possible that our souls can only love one person each lifetime? What if there are multiple soul mates or, more radical still, what if the idea of a soul mate is completely wrong? Perhaps the truth is that we confine ourselves to these societal norms just to keep a certain level of control over our lives. But I was living proof that conformism rarely makes for a happy life.

The universe was now teaching me something precious. I continued to deeply love Catherine, but I felt love for Susana, too. It made me wonder…what if this notion of soul mate isn't for everyone? What if some of us are meant to romantically love multiple people over the course of a lifetime? Why do we label someone who has been married multiple times as failures? Perhaps some of us do use the concept of marriage in the wrong way. Yes, being married multiple times can be a sign that you have refused to see the mirrors that each partner presents and so, you just keep attracting more mirrors until you see what lies within. But what if for others, the path is really to love more than one person in a lifetime? Maybe the best we can do, when it comes to the definitions and concepts about romantic love, is charter our own path and not buy into the collective consciousness that pulls in one direction or another. We all have unique paths in life and they are all blessed.

08/23/13
Me: Father, what is Susana's role in my life? She was a lovely, but

189

unexpected gift!

Father: Through her you will really learn how to love without attachment.

Me: How and why her?

Father: She has entered your life at exactly the perfect time. Again, Heaven's timing is always perfect. She is a strong light, a beautiful being. She's a free spirit. Think of her as a firefly. Fireflies illuminate the night sky with their beautiful light, but if you try to grab them, they quickly fly away from you. The way to get close to a firefly is to gently lay your hand out and patiently wait for the firefly to land on it. When she does, you keep your hand open, enjoy the close up view and connection with the firefly, but she is still free to leave if she so chooses. Gently holding your hand open...that is the key. If you try to catch a firefly, she will quickly lose all her beauty and light. Loving without attachment is exactly that, my child—holding a gentle open hand and enjoying every minute of the company you have with someone. That is what Susana will teach you and it is one of the most important lessons you have for this lifetime. Your energies have attracted each other because you both have something to learn from each other in order to grow.

Me: What will I teach her?

Father: That is not your concern. It is between her and I. Focus instead on you. Release this fear, my child. Everything will be okay. Actually, everything IS okay.

BOOM

32 LOVING WITHOUT ATTACHMENT

When it came to romantic relationships, I've always operated under an all-or-nothing model: I either kept people miles away from my heart or held on to them with an iron grip. The little devil on my shoulder had been whispering for years that eventually everyone will leave me. And I had always believed him. But so what? What is it about this possibility that has always terrified me into panic? The truth is, we face the most important events in our lives alone. We suffer alone. We die alone. We are born alone. Every single life event is lived alone. With every unbearable death and loss I'd experienced, my soul knew the pain must be felt alone, but my ego squirmed at the very thought. We travel through life, filling it with love and laughter and joy. Yet when you die, even if you're surrounded by those who love you best in the world, you are going through the process alone. They are witnesses to it, but you experience it in a way they cannot. And for many of us, the idea that we are essentially alone is utterly terrifying.

I sat down and started to think this through. If my little devil was right and everyone eventually leaves me, does that mean we are destined to experience life alone? What if alone really means 'not attached.' BOOM...a light bulb went off in my head and I immediately recalled something Anthony De Mello once said. You cannot love until you are alone. There it was. The fundamental truth here is that we all walk our paths alone. And that's exactly how the universe is meant to be experienced! We live out individual experiences on this earth and the people around us add texture, beauty and love. We are not meant to be lonely, because that is an emotional state of yearning caused by isolation. Aloneness is simply a state of existence. We are all individuals, like grains of sand. Together, we may make up a beach or desert, but we exist alone, in our own right. Even surrounded by loved ones, we should always be aware and accept our aloneness. Why? Because when you do, you cease to need anything or anyone else in order to be happy and you will never be lonely.

I started thinking about the analogy JCS had shared with me. Imagine you are standing in the middle of a beautiful field at night. The sky is filled with glorious fireflies, buzzing around you in an endless dance of light. One firefly can represent your spouse; another your job; yet another your material possessions. The way to live without attachment is keep an open hand and enjoy the firefly once it lands, or accept the possibility that no firefly will land at all. An open hand also means that if a firefly lands, it is still free to leave. With an open hand, you are adaptable to all that comes your way. And that means being open and flexible about love, too. When a firefly (or a person) lands in your life, you can love with clear-eyed intensity because they may be there for a reason, a season or a lifetime. Knowing that, your mind focuses on the present and every joyful second of interaction. If you live with an open hand, you will stop putting conditions on your happiness. You will stop saying "I can only be happy if I have money" or "I am unhappy without my spouse." You'll also stop identifying with the fireflies in your life. By just enjoying each firefly for what it is, you don't build your own self-worth around their presence. They are what they are and you are what you are, 100 percent precious and wonderful, regardless of who or what comes into your life.

For four years, I held on to Catherine with an iron fist, because I was afraid of losing her. I defined my self-worth by her presence, by my job and my education. I had suffocated her. My attachment to her meant she had to subscribe to how I needed her to behave, if I was to be happy. If she was 'too competitive' or 'worked too much', I used those interpretations to guide her behavior and to prove that she loved me. When she left me, I fought her decision, instead of respecting it. I didn't do that because of my love for her. I did it because without her, my cup would be empty and I would be alone.

In the weeks after we met, I came to realize just how apt the firefly metaphor was when it came to Susana. Every time I got close, she would panic and run away. I would feel a deep sense of rejection. I still believed an empty hand meant I wasn't good enough. And so, I meditated daily and allowed myself to feel this rejection wound deeply. I was so thankful for Susana and who she was because she was exactly what I needed in order to evolve. It was only by feeling my wound that I came face to face with another part of me that still needed to see the light of day. I was being rejected by yet another person I loved. My ego was desperately trying to rebuild the dam. It was trying to force me to close my heart. My little devil was whispering, "Close your heart before someone else rejects you." But I would not allow it. I would sit in meditation and cry if I had to, I would feel the unyielding force of this pain deeply, but I would not close my heart. As I went through this process of holding my heart gently, no matter what happened to it, I was overwhelmed with joy at the "new Tina." I could be hurt and my heart poked, but I could also smile and be joyful throughout it.

After some time passed, I found myself on the phone with Susana. It was a painful talk, but I also experienced an epic breakthrough, too. In our two-hour conversation, I began to notice just how deeply she relied on me emotionally. She was living in a new environment, far away from her family and friends on mainland. And I knew how life on the islands can be isolating. I had become her rock, the person she went to when she felt off balance. Yet at the same time, I was also rocking her off balance in other ways. I knew what she felt for me, but still she resisted. She had been going through her own internal storms ever since I entered her life and I was beginning to understand what my role was in her evolution. Even so, whatever her internal struggles, they hurt me in the process. As we spoke, she made it brutally clear she did not feel the same way for me. "She's lying," I thought. Yet, it didn't matter. In this moment, I felt another separation in me. My consciousness was again assuming the role of observer, just as it had the day Catherine told me it was over. As Susana was talking, I realized that I was not being treated as I wished to be or how I deserved to be treated. Her storms were hers to deal with. It wasn't my business to interfere. I deserved to be treated like gold, not an emotional crutch. I saw that I was repeating my old pattern of giving all of myself to another, with nothing in return. My soul whispered, "You still don't fully love yourself."

Strengthened by this realization, I gently bid goodbye. I knew what I had to do. I would walk away without judgment or resentment. I had spent weeks chasing a firefly, because I believed an empty hand meant I was worthless. It was only when I heard her unpleasantness on the phone that I realized how priceless I was. My love for her wouldn't change, but I also loved and respected myself, too. Old Tina would have continued chasing the firefly even if she didn't reciprocate. Old Tina would have continued to allow herself to be mistreated because in the end, she always believed herself to be deserving of it. Evolved, beautiful, spiritually aware Tina was a whole different beast. She understood the lesson of non-attachment. She understood what it really meant to hold her hand gently open in a field full of fireflies. And yet, like fireflies, we are constantly in motion. Rarely do we stand still long enough for a firefly to land on us. We walk, run and dance through life. A firefly is still free to land on my open hand, but I am also free to choose whether or not it stays. We don't need to allow a firefly to remain if they wound us. When Susana chose her path, I would gently blow her off my hand and continue my own beautiful dance.

This was truly self-love and self-respect. And yet we all have those people who are hard to leave behind, no matter how damaging they are to our wellbeing. We deserve so much more that what they offer. We deserve love and kindness and respect. It's up to us to choose them. In your life, if you see someone who causes you pain, remember that you are dancing through a field of fireflies and you absolutely have the choice about which ones get to stay on your hand. There will be moments where you need great courage to ask a firefly to leave. But you have it within you to say the words.

33 HEADING UP AND OVER

My trip home to Portugal was now coming to an end. I was heading back to California. But there was one last person who would reappear in my life before I left. The day before my departure, I waited for my mom in her car. Staring out the window and thinking nothing in particular, I heard a car pull up beside me. I glanced over and panicked. It was Susana. She rolled down her window. "Funny to find you right at this moment! What are you doing? Do you want to come on a road trip with me? I'm going to pick up my friends who went for a hike." Obviously I said yes.

Driving along the hydrangea-lined roads, I was quiet but Susana wanted to talk. She had been seeing someone else and was curious about my reaction. She also respected my "extra sense" and pried me for any details from beyond. "Why have you both shown up in my life at the same time?" I smiled and looked out the window. "Perhaps the universe is showing you a contrast." She was confused. "What kind of contrast?" I paused, searching for the right words. "Well, besides the fact that he's a man and I'm a woman, perhaps life is showing you the difference between what the ego wants and what the heart wants." Silence. She received the message. I already knew I was in her life to show her what real love is, but those were details I left out of our conversations. I was learning to use my skill of connection to other realms wisely. I was not supposed to use any information for the wrong reasons. I was learning the ethics of being a medium and embraced them wholeheartedly.

When we arrived at the pre-determined pick-up spot on the other side of the island, Susana's friends were late. "Let's walk for a bit," I said, wanting to enjoy my last minutes of alone time with this beautiful soul. Even through all her internal struggles, I could see her essence and I loved it. We sat on the rocks looking out to the ocean. "I think we're too close to the water," she warned. But I didn't listen. "We'll be fine." Just then, a massive wave broke over us. We laughed and in that moment, we were happy. We sat there in silence for a little while, looking out at the magnificent expanse. Then I broke the silence. "Why do you think the universe has brought us together today?" She smiled. "I don't know." Then she held my hand and we sat a little longer before her friends arrived. In all honesty, I didn't even know the answer to what I had asked her. What was the universe doing? My firefly was right there; sitting on my open hand. And yet I was leaving the very next day. What the hell was happening?

The next day, stupefied by jetlag, I heard JCS's voice just as I was falling asleep. *Rest, my child, for you will have many decisions to make very soon. Important decisions that require you to be intensely in the present moment.* Exhausted, I fell asleep before I was able to think about what I had heard.

A few days later, I drove to central California for a family weekend getaway with Aunt Eva. As I walked the long stretch of white sand beach at Pismo Beach, I had two separate thoughts in my mind. The first was JCS's message to me, the second was a request from a friend who'd heard about my ability to talk to dead people. I had no idea what JCS meant by having important decisions to make very soon. Since I had learned about the time delay Heaven seemed to operate on, it didn't make any sense to worry. Actually, worrying never makes sense because it's a sign we're living in our melodramas, not the present moment. The second topic intrigued me. My friend Kim had asked me if I could possibly speak to her mother, who had passed away after an extended illness. Conversations with Kim and Courtney during their island honeymoon had sparked her interest in my work and Kim was curious. Yet, her request made me nervous. I was absolutely confident that I could talk to the other side, but my conversations had taken place with souls whom I was deeply connected to.

A few days later, I sat down in meditation and asked JCS for some help. His response was quick: *You can speak to anyone. Why don't you try to travel to Heaven like you used to do when we first started talking?* I could feel JCS wink when He said this, so I figured it was worth a shot. I asked Kim for some pictures of her mother where I could clearly see her eyes. Then I sat at my computer and practiced some self-kindness before opening the attachments I had just received. "It's okay if I can't do it," I said gently to myself. I was a bit concerned because I hadn't known Kim for very long, and we never discussed her mother. I could sense it was a painful topic, so I had always shied away from asking any questions. As I opened Kim's attachments, I felt a wave of emotions take hold of my body. I began to cry. There she was, smiling and looking into the camera with her blue eyes. They were greyish in tone and revealed her soul to me right away. Her face was round and her hair short, but stylish. Blonde. I said her name out loud. "Myrna." Immediately, I felt her presence in the room. It was quite overwhelming and beautiful. I could feel her soul energy deep in my stomach and a deep feeling of love overtook my body. I felt her love for her daughter. It was very palpable.

With her face in my mind, I laid down on the floor, closed my eyes and put on my headphones. The music playing was a meditation melody I'd used countless times before. I felt myself ascend into my field of tall grass. I was in Heaven. In the middle of the field was a lovely bench, facing away from me and toward the horizon. I slowly approached it from behind and saw that there was someone waiting for me. It was Myrna. I could see her as clearly as if she were standing right in the same room as me. She looked over and smiled as I sat down next to her.

08/19/13
Me: Hi Myrna!
M: Hello, my dear! Thank you for coming.
Me: You look a little sad. What is wrong?
M: You know, when I was down there, I didn't always communicate well with my daughter. I loved her so very much, but I sometimes had a hard time showing that. When I got sick, our relationship deepened, but I wished I had nurtured it better when I was well. Her father and I made some mistakes, but they were all part of our path.
We sat in silence for a little while and then she got up from the bench and ran her fingers through her hair.
M: What do you think of my hairdo dear?
Me: It's fabulous, Myrna.
She then started dancing around the field.
M: You know, I was never a good dancer down there, but up here I can master anything! What do you think?
Me: You look lovely dancing, Myrna.
M: Tell my daughter I am happy and well, and that one day she will be here dancing with me.
Me: I will.
M: Thank you so much for coming to talk to me. You have been such a gift in my daughter's life. I was there on their wedding day, it was beautiful. For years I wanted to communicate that her [first] marriage was not right. Something wasn't right. But now she has found her love and that makes me so happy.
She sat next to me on my bench again.
M: Will you come back and talk to me more? I have more to share.
Me: Yes, Myrna, I will.

M: Thanks, dear.
BOOM

When I emerged from my travel, I was really confused. What kind of conversation was that? Was I even seeing and hearing things correctly? Although the conversation didn't make much sense to me and wasn't really detailed at all, I decided to transcribe it and send it over to Kim. At least it seemed like a good first reading. "Hey Kim," I wrote, "I have no idea if I actually spoke to your mom, but I hope this conversation makes sense to you." An hour later, I received a response. "I believe you did speak to my mom," she wrote. "I cried for about 20 minutes." It turns out the weird aspects of my conversation with Myrna served as proof. According to Kim, her mother was always the first person to jump onto the dance floor at any event. She also owned about 50 wigs and constantly asked people what they thought of her hair. I was amazed. It made me feel more and more confident in my skill and all the spiritual work I had done in the past months.

A day after the reading with Myrna, I found myself immersed in real world problems. One of my student loan lenders had decided that I was not eligible for a six month grace period that is usually allowed when students return to school. I had graduated just three months earlier, yet I was told I was now delinquent on my payments. I tried for an hour on the phone to understand how I was magically considered ineligible for a grace period. It then dawned on me how screwed I was: I had no job, no money and no way to make repayments. After hanging up, I felt the familiar knot in my stomach. What on earth was I going to do now? Just as I was beginning to ponder this question, an email popped up in my inbox, entitled, "Interested in an academic position at a university?" It was from a recruiter who had come upon my resume and found it impressive. Still feeling numb from my stressful phone conversation, I replied that I could be interested, but wanted to know more. I loved teaching and had previously considered the possibility of becoming a university professor. But as I spoke to the recruiter on the phone, something in me didn't click. I just knew in my core that my path was different now. My bank account was telling me 'take the job' but my soul was saying 'your job is your book.' After thinking this over, I wrote to the recruiter.

Hello Roger;

Thank you so much for reaching out. I feel that this is not the right fit for me, but appreciate your kind words and hope you can find the right person soon!

Warm Wishes,

Christina

As I hit send, I felt a momentary surge of fear. I walked outside, looked to the skies and thought, "Holy shitballs!! I just turned down a great job possibility right at the time when I need money the most! Have I gone completely insane?" After my mini panic attack however, I felt a deep joy bubble to the surface. I had turned down a job prospect that wasn't part of my path. That felt *good.* I had allowed my soul to command me and although the destination was as yet uncertain, I had faith! True, my bills were overdue and I had no way of paying them, but I just felt a deep certainty that everything was going exactly as it should. The very next day, I received a call from my lender. It appears that after reviewing my account, they had decided to waive my overdue days and bring my account current. They also decided to give me one more month until my first payment was due. "Wow, thank you so much," I managed to utter, stunned. How on earth had that happened?

Oh boy, the twists and turns that life can take sometimes. Right after turning down a job prospect and dealing with my student debt, I had another issue to resolve and this one was consuming me. During the process of separation, Catherine was clear that she didn't want to keep our Great Dane, Xena. I was glad she decided because I deeply loved my big, slobbery baby, who had been with me during so many difficult times. I had left her behind in DC for a few months while I sorted out my life, but what on earth was I going to do now? I was staying at my Aunt Eva's house in California, but had no intention of living there permanently. I love the West Coast for visiting, but I didn't sense I was supposed to settle down there again. And I certainly didn't sense a move back to DC. That was out of the question. Where would I go with a cow-sized dog? I had no financial means to keep her and no home in which to house her. I took a breath as the fear started creeping in. It was time to meditate.

Take her home. My eyes popped open immediately as soon as I heard the voice whispering in my head. I started talking out loud. "Take Xena home as in...the Azores? How in bloody hell am I supposed to do that?" Yes, I was actually arguing out loud with no one. But then I sensed something deeper. If the universe wanted my cow of a dog to be moved to the islands, then things would roll smoothly. I knew that life would make things happen when it was ready. The universe assists us when we listen. So I got up from meditation and went straight to my laptop. I wanted to send Catherine an email, to test the idea of taking Xena to the Azores. I had no idea how that would happen, but I asked anyway. Five minutes later I received a reply. "I think it's a great idea and I'll pay for your expenses." Okay then. I guess that solves one major problem!

And that is how I found myself back on my island, a mere two weeks after returning to California. The whole episode was one of intense preparation, logistics and pure flow. Let's just say it's not that easy to get a beast like Xena from the States to my island in the middle of the Atlantic. But life helped, things went smoothly, and my big puppy girl arrived safe and sound. The whole situation was surreal to me and I was having difficulty centering myself. One day I'm in CA meditating and few days later I'm back on my island. I'm back on my island...where the woman I loved lived. What other twists did the universe have in store for me?

34 SURRENDER

Zen. As a word, it comes as loaded as a baked potato. It conjures up images of Buddhist monks meditating, prayer wheels, singing bowls and incense. They are centered and calm, but how do we stay that way amidst the noisy cacophony of every day chaos? How do we stay calm when everything is falling apart? Let's start with how we interpret things, good and bad. When I say chaos, it sounds inherently bad because chaos means "a state of utter confusion or disorder; a total lack or organization or order." It is the unexpected and generally speaking, people are not huge fans of the unexpected, because we operate under the illusion of control. Chaos and control just don't mingle and our egos know it.

Now, walk through this exercise with me. Think about what's going on in your life and think about all the things you've labelled 'good' or 'bad.' Maybe you're in debt. Perhaps your marriage is falling apart. It could be that you're having trouble with your kids, your boss or best friend. Now, remove the labels. Think to yourself, "Everything is exactly as it is supposed to be right now." How absolutely transformative. When you stop labeling things as 'good' or 'bad', you open up a space that is miraculous. It's a space inside of you that is called 'surrender.' And in that space, you accept everything that is here, right now.

Surrender is a central theme in Buddhism, although some have mistakenly interpreted it to mean passivity. The truth is that when you cease to label things and events, you surrender to what is. You surrender to things that are entering your life now. This is not passive. Passivity occurs when you lie in bed with the covers over your head for days on end and refuse to engage in life. Surrender is the humble act of saying, "Here is an event and since I am aware I cannot control it, I will accept its arrival instead." You're not avoiding events or letting them railroad you. Rather, you are truly engaging with what is coming your way. Surrender and acceptance are really the only way you can profoundly engage with life. When you create that space of surrender, you become instantly more capable of responding to life's events in a truly powerful way.

Think of surrendering as a trampoline. A trampoline propels you higher if its surface has more give and surrenders to your weight. But that surrendering is almost instantaneously transformed into an awesome power of propulsion. The more flexibility a trampoline has, the higher you fly. The same applies to surrendering to life's events. When something painful happens and you say no to it, it's like jumping from a concrete floor. If you say yes to all events that come your way, even the most painful ones, you will find yourself jumping on a flexible trampoline. Your surrender will be instantly transformed into a powerful response. Your response may end up being something internal and not even visible to the outside world, but it will be powerful nonetheless.

This is all easy enough to describe, but how does it work in a practical sense, amidst sorrow and grief? Let's imagine you've just learned that someone you love deeply is gravely ill and not likely to live. Surrendering to the reality would look something like this.

Step 1. This is the reality and I cannot change it.

Step 2. I surrender to it and make space in me for the event to pass through.

Step 3: I deeply feel what the event causes inside of me.

Step 4: I breathe and melt like a candle under the heat of a flame.

Step 5: I respond to the event.

Many of us can't even do Step 1 because we are in so much pain. We fight the fact that our loved one is dying. Grief can make us irrational, because we can't fight something that is happening. But let's say we get through to Step 2. At this point, you must feel the emotions the event triggers. This is the step most of us run from and is the main reason why we end up saying 'no' to life events. Deeply feeling what the death of a loved will be like is excruciating, but in order to live fully and with an open heart, you must learn how to sit with and feel what events cause inside you.

Step 3 is the most important because it prepares you for Step 5. Do you think you can properly respond to a life event if you can't even acknowledge how that event makes you feel? It takes so much courage to sit with your pain and surrender to its unyielding force. It takes a strength far superior to a warrior's to embrace pain and cradle it gently like a newborn baby. Yet feeling the pain is the only way to prepare you for an appropriate response. Being able to master this step can make a profound difference in your life. It can mean that a father who suddenly lost his beloved child, for example, can find joy again in life instead of losing himself to substance abuse or depression. Allowing myself to deeply feel the loss of my wife had caused the opening of my heart. Sitting with and feeling all my past pain had finally opened a space for me to truly love. Once you live Step 3, this is where breathing at Step 4 can come to your rescue. When a life event causes internal discomfort, I've made it a practice to breathe deeply and feel my body melting. I bring the power of my awareness to my breath and to the feeling of relaxation. That simple practice of "melting" into a life event works wonders. It's a sign of ultimate surrender to what is.

09/15/13

JCS: Your fear has returned in force my child, hasn't it?
I began to cry.
Me: Yes Father...it has been difficult to break out of this lately. This fear is so old...I actually have no idea where it comes from.
JCS: You know, you're not just feeling your own. You are feeling the fears of those you love. Here with your family, you feel their fear and return to an old pattern of yours: the pattern of wanting to carry someone else's pain. Do you remember when I told you a while back that you needed to learn to just bear witness to someone else's pain, without wanting to take it away? Well, fear is a part of pain. You panic when you feel the fear of those around you and you try to control outside events so those you love do not have to feel their fear. But I have already alerted you to the fact that you cannot do that. You cannot carry someone else's pain. My child, you must learn to just be with someone's pain. Just be.
Me: I feel instantly better when I meditate. But then the fear returns. I have no idea why.
JCS: I want to talk about something important again: meditation. Do you remember when I said you could meditate even in the middle of a rock concert? I said that because it's important for you to understand that the connection with Heaven must be constant in these times that you all face down there. To meditate in the traditional way, sitting just as you are now, continues to be important, but you cannot spend the day like that. The meditation that I talk about is more simply a connection with Heaven. You must be constantly connected with Heaven right now. And how do you do that? By living intensely in the present moment. You cannot remain connected when you live of imagined scenarios or let your fear overtake you. The meditation that I am talking about can take place at any time or place during your day. When you feel your ego begin to imagine things or when your fear becomes very strong, just stop and breathe deeply. Breathe deeply and do what you wrote in your book, melt like candle wax under a flame. And return to the present moment, to whatever situation presents itself in the now. You may have to do this one hundred times a day and

that's fine. This is the most important type of meditation I want you to do right now. Breathe deeply and return to the present. Only in the present will your connection to Heaven be strong and constant. I love you very much, my child.
BOOM

I sat alone for a while and pondered the first part of this conversation. I felt that one of the most important evolutionary lessons was to learn how to bear witness to someone's pain. I quite simply did not know how to do that, aside from wishing I could take pain away whenever I saw it. Perhaps this was a trait ingrained from early childhood experiences or perhaps I brought it from another lifetime. It doesn't matter. The fundamental truth was that I panicked when those I loved suffered. In this case, it was my mother's condition that was deeply affecting me and I didn't know how to break my old pattern.

My mother has always suffered with physical ailments since she was a child, such as mysterious fevers, early arthritis and spinal deformities. She had always been in some form of physical pain since I could remember. Yet through the years, she just kept going. But there comes a time in all of our lives when our bodies no longer listen as intently to our willpower. In my mother's case, a combination of arthritis and a herniated disk in her back meant she could barely walk some days. As she reached her pain tolerance, she would become angrier than I had ever seen her. It was hard for me to observe my mother's struggle and inability to surrender to her body's limits. But it was horrendous to witness her pain, knowing that I could do very little to help. I suspect this was the root of my newly returned anxiety. I resisted the idea that my mother was reaching her limit. I was refusing to face the fact that I could not help her on this journey. In the past, I would deal with other's pain by trying to alleviate it through my medical skills or, if all else failed, ignore it. But this time, it dawned on me that the most profound thing I could do was to put my hand out and say, "I am here for you." It used to seem so trivial and inconsequential, but now I knew how that simple act could change someone's life.

09/16/13

Me: Father, I've done so much work, but I don't know how to lose this fear that makes me suffer so much.

JCS: You know, your fear comes from past lives, not just this one. But you are focusing on it with a fighting energy. You are fighting your fear and you already know that fighting against something rarely gets you anywhere. Do you know what is necessary? Surrender. Acceptance. Accept that this fear is a part of you and give it room to express itself. Look at your fear like a child having a tantrum. Stroke her hair and simply say 'It's okay.' Be with your fear. Feel it deeply. That is when it will lose its power over you. Now, when your body feels ill for reasons you do not comprehend, you immediately panic and let the child turn into a monster. You let your fear take over your body. But remember that the child will only turn into a monster if you let her! If you have compassion for the child, if you love her as a part of you, she will quieten. Accept all parts of yourself openly my child. Now come on! Lighten up, my pearl! What is lacking in this precise moment?

Me: Nothing, Father. Nothing.

BOOM

35 SEEING THE PAST

I have lived in a state of fear and panic for most of my life, so it is quite impossible to describe the liberation I felt as the fear slowly dissipated. The universe was teaching me how paradise doesn't really exist and that the road of evolution brings with it some slight bumps. I hadn't realized just how wonderful I truly felt until I returned home for the second time and found myself immersed in panic again. The return of my fear was also a good indicator that there were plenty of aspects in my life where I still operated with my old mental models. I sat in silence for a while and let a question float in the air: "What am I so afraid of?" Well, off the top of my head, the first answer was that I was worried about my financial situation. My little devil was quick to chime in. "You're broke, have bills to pay, and you just turned down a good job prospect. Dumbass." The little devil was probably saying something that my family or friends would say, had I told them of the job prospect. Yes, I was doing something that others would probably easily deem irresponsible or stupid. I should be looking for a steady job in my field of expertise. That's how life is supposed to work right?

The problem is that I knew my path was going to be

something vastly different than I had anticipated. There would be nothing steady or normal about it. Yet, although I had this certainty, it was very difficult for me to open up with others when asked where I was going to work. There was something in that question that caused my stomach to knot. I sat in meditation with that question, trying to delve as deeply as I could into this fear about my financial situation and recognition that my new path was completely financially uncertain, especially in the short term. "Breathe deeply and melt like candle wax under a flame." That seemed to be my new motto. And with it, self-kindness and the recognition that I was simply feeling a bump in the road. Everything was just right.

One day not long after, I was on a run in the mountains with Xena and my mom's old dog, Tiger. Xena now had a best friend and every single day we would run together in the breathtaking scenery. I had never seen my dog this happy. She was free, joyful. "How will I ever take her off this island when I eventually move? It will break her heart." I wondered. Suddenly, my mental conversations gave way to the familiar knot in my stomach. My anxiety was back. And with it came a flash of annoyance. "I've been doing so much work, but this fear just won't leave me!" I powered through the familiar chest tightness and found myself talking out loud. "Can someone please help me understand why I have this deep fear and where it comes from?" Instantly, I felt a numbness take over my body. I knew what it was. Someone on the other side wanted to talk to me. I turned around and started running back home. By the time I walked in the door, I already had a feeling the person waiting for me was my paternal grandmother, Vó.

09/17/13
As soon as I closed my eyes and entered my field, I began to cry. I ran to Vó.
Vó: It's okay, my child, everything is okay. All is as it should be.
Me: I don't know what else to do to lose this fear that takes over my body

sometimes. I am terrified of dying and have no idea why!
She gently stroked my hair and we walked over to my bench to talk. Vó
held my hand and shared some of her wonderful energy with me. I felt my
body calm immediately.
Vó: This fear is not from your current life. Would like to see where it
comes from?
Me: Yes!
We started walking across my field, but the grass suddenly turned into
sand and I could see we were in an arena of some sort, like a big old
stadium. I was a tall and muscular man, with no shoes, standing in the
middle of this stadium. I could feel Roman energy as if I was living in a
gladiator movie. I felt horrible pain in my body and was bleeding profusely.
The stadium was full of people, screaming things I could not understand. I
was surrounded by armored soldiers riding in open horse carriages and they
held large chains with spiked balls in the end. They charged toward me
and hit my body repeatedly with the sharp balls. I could feel the bones in
my body break, especially in my chest. The flesh was being torn from my
body with each successive strike and I saw myself fall to the ground
multiple times. I was a very strong man, but defenseless against these
soldiers and their weapons. I then saw myself thrown in a cell, dying alone
and in terrible pain. It was at this moment that I realized I had an
intellectual disability. I had the body of a man but the intellect of a child. I
think I died in that cell alone, my body broken to pieces. My child-like
brain could not understand why anyone would want to hurt me and I was
so afraid. I cried alone and in the darkness of that cell. It felt like I was
crying for my mother.
Vó: Okay, my child, that's enough. Now do you see why you are so
terrified of dying? But it's over, my angel, and now you are living another
life. Come now, it's time to go. You have seen enough for today.
Vó held my hand and we left that horrible place. We entered my field
again and sat at our bench.
Vó: It's time to release this fear now. Accept it and do as Jesus says.
Know that you are never alone, we are always here to help. Anytime you
need us, we are here. I love you very much.
BOOM

09/18/13

Me: Father, I feel like I'm being energetically attacked. My body does not feel well at all.

JCS: You know, you are again approaching the situation from a fighting energy. But the reality is of love, not of battle. I want you to think with more love, my child. Your light is visible to all. You are like a warm fire on a dark, cold night. Everyone wants to huddle around the fire to warm their hands and see each other. There is a lot of love around a fire. The reason you do not feel well is because the souls that wish to get close to your fire are precisely the ones that have not seen light in a very long time. They do not wish to harm you, my child. Have compassion and love for darkness, my pearl.

I began to cry.

Me: But will I always have to feel this way?

JCS: Of course not! Don't be so dramatic! There are ways to protect yourself. Tell me this: the last time you were home you did not feel this way, did you?

Me: No, the last time I felt wonderful!

JCS: Exactly. So what has changed?

Me: My fear has returned.

JCS: There you have it! As you can see, you are responsible for maintaining your aura. You are each responsible for what you feel and the energies you emanate. I know this trip is not as easy as the last, but remember that you are not on vacation. You are here to do some very important work, and it is not only about your love life. Have you noticed that it was here, on this island, in this house, in your very bedroom, that you developed some of the most toxic patterns of this life? And it is here that you must transmute that energy once and for all. You cannot leave one single stone unturned. This work is arduous and needs your complete attention. Go into your past, feel your pain, be still with it, and let it go. Be free of it all. New energy, my pearl...new energy. Don't forget, I'm always with you. Always. All you need to do is call for me.

BOOM

He was right, of course. How did I miss that my toxic patterns had all started on the island? As I sat outside digesting another one of JCS's messages, I reviewed my life. I left the island at 17. "That was really young," I thought. My pain and panic had been so strong, that I literally ran away just a few months after my father had died. Outwardly, I pretended that my move to the US was coming from a foundation of strength. Everyone around me admired my tenacity, my ambition. Yet, little did they know that I was literally running away from life! But on this day, sitting outside and looking out at that immense ocean I so loved, I finally realized why my anxiety returned whenever I came home.

My house, my island, my mother and brother, the stretch of Atlantic Ocean I could see from my bedroom window, they were all triggers. They triggered old pain and that pain caused fear, panic. The biggest wounds of my life were acquired in this island paradise and yet, year after year, I refused to look at them. "Go into your past, feel your pain, be still with it, and let it go. Be free of it all." I was finally acknowledging the biggest wound of my life, where my profound fear of loss was born. I had talked about my past, but only glossed the surface, the events and people, but not the pain they caused. Being home and having my anxiety return was actually the most miraculous thing that could have ever happened. That anxiety and panic was there to remind me of something. I was distracted with the fear that they brought and coursed through my veins. Yet underneath that strong emotion was a gentle whisper that said, "You have something unresolved to deal with." I decided to dive under the surface of the water and see just how big my iceberg was.

"You cannot leave one single stone unturned," Jesus had told me. Right. I would deconstruct my panic attacks one layer at a time. I wanted to know why I held onto so much fear. Was it past life trauma, current life trauma, chakra disturbances, a biochemical imbalance, a heart problem? Over the years, I had consulted various physicians, but the recommendation was always the same—take this pill and learn to relax. Yet I always had a feeling that pharmaceuticals would only quieten the symptom, not deal with the underlying problem. There had to be another way.

The attacks usually started when I felt my heart rate increase or when my body experienced the many weird sensations I cannot explain. A sequence of thoughts that made the panic worse would follow: "Your heart is going to stop," "you're going to pass out," "you need to escape," "you're going to die alone." In the past, I had dealt with these thoughts by focusing the flashlight of consciousness on the intense fear I was feeling. My mind would zero in on it to the exclusion of all else. "What you focus on expands," Wayne Dyer once said. My little devil was ramping up my panic and I was letting him. It was time to change things up a little.

The next day, I was having lunch with my family, at our favorite little ocean-side restaurant. We were eating out in the warm sun and hearing the waves break just a few feet away. I was sitting at the table with my mom, one of her sisters, and a family friend. Everything was perfectly normal. Suddenly, I felt the fear return. My heart rate started slowly increasing, my chest tightened and I had the urge to run to the bathroom. Then, I remembered my own advice: watch the movie, don't become part of it. My fear was the movie and it was trying very hard to pull my awareness to it. I forced myself to sit there. I talked to my mother about something trivial. I focused my attention on the present moment and the fact that I was sitting comfortably at a restaurant with my family. As the conversation progressed, my fear dissipated. I was living my own words.

As the days progressed, I revived the technique again and again. I would be washing dishes or driving down the street and feel fear. And I would overcome it. Slowly, I started feeling deep joy and gratitude. I was profoundly grateful for my anxiety. I was grateful that this fear was a part of me because through it, I was learning yet another important lesson.

Focusing your attention intensely on the present moment is hard enough. Focusing whilst in the midst of utter panic is excruciatingly difficult. But if I could do it during a panic attack, that meant I could now do it every single day of my life! And that brought a huge smile to my face.

36 TURNING EVERY SINGLE STONE

09/22/13
JCS: This is a very important lesson for you in this lifetime: Love does not demand; it has no expectations; it does not wish to control. Love is freedom. And love is also patient. Remember: patiently hold an open hand and wait for the firefly to land on it. The firefly will land.
BOOM

With all of the other lessons I was learning since returning home, none was more difficult than loving without attachment. My return home had brought panic to the woman I loved. I tried mentally to understand Susana's fears. Was she panicking because she wasn't very comfortable with her sexuality? Was she afraid of what she felt for me? Every single time I tried to get close to her, she would run away. Rejection. I felt that wound so often since being back home. Yet this time things were different. I had a deep understanding now that everything we encounter in life is showing us a mirror that reflects something about ourselves. I was still chasing the firefly and trying to grab her. It was tremendously difficult to learn how to keep my hand gently open for the firefly to land in freedom. And yes, it was all a beautiful miracle. I was in love with someone who had her own wounds and those wounds were teaching me something about myself. It reminded me of a quote I love, by spiritual teacher, Ram Dass: "We're all just walking each other home." How beautiful. Susana was showing me the path to my own evolution of consciousness. She was being my guru. She was "walking me home." JCS had already told me that loving without attachment was an important milestone for me to achieve in this lifetime. I was ready.

09/24/13

JCS: You know, the best way to help your brothers and sisters transform is with humility, compassion and questions! A question works like a seed that will later turn into a beautiful rose. Strategic questions are like seeds in the human mind. Statements are sometimes too strong, especially for those with ingrained patterns of behavior. Questions are softer, tenderer. They make people think and that is a very important step in human transformation. Think of an ingrained pattern like a rock. Statements transform the rock by breaking it. Questions transform the rock like water does...gently over time. As you already know, breaking a rock can cause a lot of suffering. But water does not hurt, it causes transformation without suffering. If you want to continue on this journey of being a spiritual guide, you must always remember to be water. You must speak to your brothers and sisters gently, with compassion. And always remember to use questions like seeds that will one day turn into roses!
BOOM

I understood on a basic level what JCS was saying. For most of my life, I had chosen to change minds by the force of affirmations. As I grew, I became harder, less tender. I knew this wasn't the way to change hearts and minds, but I was unable to soften because I barely knew why I had hardened in the first place. Mercifully, when my world fell apart, I finally decided to let pain soften me, and now I understood how to be 'water.' But how could I help others break their ingrained patterns when I was still struggling with mine?

I was working on my own anxiety while JCS wanted me to be the water for others. Perhaps I could walk on hot coals, just as I was teaching others how to do so. Yet how do we break these patterns that are sometimes with us over multiple lifetimes and cause so much suffering in our lives? Where do we find the courage to first identify the pattern and then choose once and for all to do something different? And even if we are capable of identifying and changing our toxic behaviors, how do we make sure they don't return a month or a year or a decade from now? Once again, JCS had the answer.

09/30/13

JCS: I need you to trust me, my treasure. I know you are suffering right now, but your metamorphosis is almost complete and the prize is great! You have a very important mission to complete on this earth and what you are feeling in your body is duality playing out. The universe is dual, as you already know. Your presence on this island right now has caused the pendulum to swing strongly toward light. But do you know what happens to a pendulum when it swings strongly to one side? It comes back and swings just as strongly to the other. That is what you are experiencing right now, a swing toward density. Just like a pendulum, the energies that are coming to you now are as strong as your light. But you know, you have something they do not. You have me! There is no opposite to me, no energy has my strength. You are my treasure and all you need to do is call for me. Nothing can escape my light. Rest, take care of your body and purify your aura. The pendulum will rest soon and your body will stop suffering. Pretty soon, your light will be so strong that very few things will affect you anymore. And the prize for all your suffering will be great. I love you, my treasure.
BOOM

The first thing I thought when I heard JCS's words today was "from your mouth to God's ears!" The previous few days had been terrible. I was physically exhausted. The anxiety had taken its toll. I really felt like I was being attacked energetically, even if JCS had already asked me to look at the situation with more love and less fight. Thankfully, my beautiful friend Sandra—or Twin as I call her—was always around in the most difficult times of my life. She sent me a link to some purifying meditations and I sat outside under the sun doing one of them. It involved visualizing a beam of light descend upon my body and letting the light envelop me.

When I opened my eyes, I felt instantly better. It was as if those bricks had been lifted from my shoulders! I sat in the sun for a while longer, trying to understand what had just happened. That beam of light had descended on my body like a warm bubble bath, surrounding me with an incredible feeling of love and warmth. I couldn't explain on a mental level what it did to me but the feelings I had were magnificent: unconditional love, peace, stillness. Connecting with that light, that to me represents God or Creator, brought a peace that melted my fears. It was like I had just been hugged by Source herself and she was whispering "I love you. Everything is okay."

10/01/13

JCS: You are focusing on your heart beat again. It scares you. I have something to show you now. It will help make sense of this fear. Ascend to your field. Someone is waiting for you.

I ascended and saw Vó waiting for me.

Vó: I want to show another one of your past lives, okay?

She smiled and held my hand. Suddenly, we were in a hospital. I was an old man, lying in bed. I couldn't breathe and felt my heart was weak. The old man got up from his bed and started walking down a hallway. He turned to me and asked me to follow him. A door opened and I saw myself in an old village. I was six or seven years old and my little friends were running around, playing in a field. They were happy, but I was not. I felt a scar in my chest and knew my heart was not normal. It felt like something I had since birth. One of my friends came up to me and grabbed my hand.

Friend: Come run with us!

Me: I can't. My mom won't let me.

I really wanted to run with them, but my heart was too weak and my mother was very protective. I felt her energy always wanting to hold me back when my little soul just wanted to run and be a normal kid.

Suddenly, I was an adult. I could see myself working in a shoe shop. I was profoundly unhappy and felt trapped in a body that couldn't move as I wished.

Fast forward again and I was an old man back at the hospital. Vó held my hand and took me back to Heaven. Once there, she stroked my hair and said with love. "You lived traumatic lives, my child. But now you are in a new life and have a magnificent road to walk. But this karma, this fear, you must let it go now. Walk your path with joy my child."
BOOM

As I emerged from this travel, I was numb. I could still feel so viscerally what that little boy and man felt. My reaction was so physical that it led me to believe that this traumatic lifetime had occurred immediately before my current one. I felt I still had his pain inside of me in this life. These trips to past lives were healing me slowly. I fully believed in reincarnation, but up until now that belief was more esoteric, and vaguely held. Yet with each trip to a past life, I learned more about my various paths and how to release pain associated with those lives. Sometimes, we prefer to ignore or reject memories. But they will remain stuck until we have the courage to relive them.

Reliving a memory and observing it without judgment releases the energy that is stuck. The pain is processed by simply seeing it and using the power of your intention to let it go. Regressions are also important because they can explain certain occurrences in your life. As a modality, regression therapy is increasingly used for thousands of patients who have not responded to other forms of traditional therapy. When you know why something is happening to you, it seems to lessen the burden on your mind. It also helps clear some old karma, too. When you emerge from a regression, you feel cleansed of the past, much like clearing the air after an argument. That is exactly how I felt as I digested this regression. Unfortunately, it didn't seem to have helped a lot in alleviating my anxiety. And then it hit me. I actually said it out loud, I was so amazed. "I'm not just attached to people," I said. "I am attached to this anxiety. It has defined me for many years and I identify with it." BOOM.

It had never dawned on me that I could identify with something that caused this much pain in my life. It wasn't just a part of me, 'anxiety' was a label that I used to navigate this world and it was used to define my worth. I had spent years fighting it, because I thought it meant I was weak. It was at this moment that I understood how ingrained this label had become and why this fear would come out most acutely when I was home. But now what? I paused for a little while in silence and then naturally said out loud, "I release you. You will no longer define me." Just like that. Sure, this fear could still be a part of me for the rest of this life and beyond. That's okay. I would give it room to express itself, as JCS had asked. But I would not let it define me anymore. I was just going to drop this fear label like I did all the others. One day at a time, with patience. Without leaving *one single stone unturned.*

This shift in understanding my fear also led me to another conclusion. We must always take responsibility for what we feel. The panic had been so acute in the weeks before the revelation that I had reverted back to a sort of victim state. I blamed past lives, old karma and trauma in this lifetime, dense energies attacking me. All of these things had conspired to create fear in me. But my ego snuck up on me again, encouraging me to use external events as an excuse to dodge responsibility for my emotions. JCS had told me that this fear was like a child having a tantrum and that it only turned into a monster if I allowed it. I always had a choice.

It was exciting to turn over another stone in my life, to let another aspect of me see the light. I was going to learn how to live in love and yet non-attached from people and everything else, including my own emotions.

37 LIFE IS A GLORIOUS MESS!

10/02/13
Me: Father, my book is finished, isn't it??
JCS: Indeed. This wasn't the ending you were expecting was it? Know that this is the beginning of a long journey, my child. Your metamorphosis is not yet complete and will continue for some time. But look at how far you've come!
Me: I surrender my body to the universe. I won't panic anymore when I feel ill. I release this karma that I have carried over multiple lives. I release it.
JCS smiled.
JCS: Good. Now go rest, my child. You deserve it.
BOOM

You were probably expecting this story to wrap up nicely, with me and Catherine reconnecting and living with our dog in a house with a white picket fence. Or maybe you wanted to read about me and Susana living happily ever after. That would be nice, but the universe has taught me that we have no control over what life sends our way and as such, we should hold lightly onto whatever comes, good or bad. All the same, there is a happy ending. My life looks so much different than I ever thought possible. My ex-wife is still my ex. Susana is still out there, being a firefly. I still struggle at times with this gift of mine.

I continue to learn the biggest lessons of my current life and share them with you—how to live with an open heart, how to love without attachment, how to bear witness to pain, and how to surrender to what life sends your way. In other words, life is a glorious mess!

For the first time in my life, I am utterly and completely open to what life sends my way. I do not wish to control the events that come and I walk my path with my beautiful heart laying gently on my open hand. I now live in a constant state of gratefulness. I am profoundly grateful for every single event that has blessed my life. And miraculously, I feel most grateful for the events that caused me the most pain. I know this seems counterintuitive, but your life will transform the very minute you are grateful for all moments, happy and sad. The more grateful you are, the more wonders will flow your way in an endless stream.

At the start of this book I asked, "What would you say to a stadium full of people?"

I have the answer now. Live with an open heart. Be open to all that comes. Be open to the gifts from above.

We are all so loved.

ENDNOTES

1- Murakami, H. (2009) What I Talk About When I Talk About Running. *Vintage; Reprint Edition.*

2- Kensinger, E. (2007) Negative Emotion Enhances Memory Accuracy. Behavioral and Neuroimaging Evidence. *Current Directions in Psychological Science*

3- Blue, L. (2008) Why do We Remember Bad Things? Interview with Matt Wilson.

4- Lehrer, J. (2012) The Forgetting Pill Erases Painful Memories Forever. *Wired.*

5- Roosevelt, E. (1937) This is My Story. *Harper & Brothers; 1st Edition*

6- Bolte Taylor, J. (2008) My Stroke of Insight. *Plume; 1 Reprint Edition.*

7- Singer, M. (2007) The Untethered Soul. *New Harbinger Publications/ Noetic Books; 1 edition.*

8- De Mello, A. (2011) The Way to Love. *Image.*

ABOUT THE AUTHOR

Energy healer and channel Christina Lopes was born in California but raised in Portugal's breathtaking Azores Islands. Educated in the United States, she spent almost a decade working as a pediatric physical therapist in New York City and Washington, DC, before a significant life event triggered her "awakening". Over the course of a year and a half, Christina experienced profound inner transformation and opened a previously closed door to her ability to communicate with Spirit. Christina holds a Doctorate Degree in Physical Therapy (PT, DPT) from New York University, and a Master's Degree in Public Health (MPH) from John's Hopkins University. She currently resides amongst trees in Portugal.

Manufactured by Amazon.ca
Bolton, ON

32070118R00136